THE BATTLE
OF THE ATLANTIC

NAVAL WARFARE FROM 1939–1945

Peter Darman, Editor

ROSEN
PUBLISHING®

New York

This edition is published in 2013 by:

The Rosen Publishing Group, Inc.
29 East 21st Street, New York, NY 10010

For Brown Bear Books Ltd:
Editorial Director: Lindsey Lowe
Senior Editor: Tim Cooke
Military Editor: Pete Darman
Children's Publisher: Anne O'Daly
Art Director: Jeni Child
Picture Manager: Sophie Mortimer

Library of Congress Cataloging-in-Publication Data

The Battle of the Atlantic: naval warfare from 1939–1945/[editor] Peter Darman.—First edition.
    pages cm.—(World War II)
Includes bibliographical references and index.
ISBN 978-1-4488-9237-2 (library binding)
1. World War, 1939–1945—Campaigns—Atlantic Ocean—Juvenile literature. I. Darman, Peter.
D770.B339 2013
940.54'293—dc23

2012026950

Manufactured in the United States of America

CPSIA Compliance Information: Batch #W13YA: For further information, contact Rosen Publishing, New York, at 1-800-237-9932

CONTENTS

CHAPTER 1
THE BATTLE OF THE ATLANTIC: 1939–1941

The Battle of the Atlantic began on September 3, 1939,
when Britain declared war on Nazi Germany, and did
not end until May 7, 1945. The campaign was the
longest and arguably the most important of the war.

Previous pages: A crew member of a Royal Navy destroyer keeps watch for German aircraft in the North Atlantic in April 1940. The destroyer is escorting a convoy of British merchant ships loaded with supplies traveling from the United States to Britain.

British Prime Minister Winston Churchill once wrote, "The only thing that ever really frightened me during the war was the U-boat peril." U-boats were German submarines (the German phrase was *Underseeboote*, or "undersea-boat") that preyed on transatlantic shipping. If Germany gained control of the Atlantic, Britain could be starved into surrender, impacting the outcome of the whole war in Europe.

The longest battle begins

When Britain declared war on Germany, it planned to use the Royal Navy to stop ships entering German ports to starve German war industries of vital resources. The Royal Navy was the largest navy in the world, with 12 battleships, 58 submarines, 7 aircraft carriers, and more than 200 cruisers and destroyers. In 1939, the German Navy, the Kriegsmarine, had just 3 battleships, 3 pocket battleships, 34 cruisers and destroyers, and 57 submarines. It could not hope to take on the British Fleet in open battle.

Kriegsmarine commander Grand Admiral Erich Raeder instead planned to focus on sinking merchant vessels carrying supplies to Britain, many of which came from North America.

Two German U-boats undergo training in the Baltic Sea. German U-boats had a devastating effect on Allied shipping.

Raeder intended to sever Britain's supply links by deploying warships far out in the Atlantic and U-boats around Britain's coast. To support the campaign, the Germans also laid mines in coastal waters and deployed long-range maritime aircraft to search for targets.

The convoy system

When the conflict broke out, Germany's planning soon paid off. *U-30* sank the British passenger liner *Athenia* just 10 hours after Britain's declaration of war. More than 110 civilians and crew were lost, including 28 U.S. citizens. It was the first act of a long, bitter campaign.

Britain's response was to adopt a convoy system in which groups of merchant ships were escorted by warships. The system had been effective in World War I (1914–1918). Britain also formed patrol groups, based around large warships such as aircraft carriers, to hunt for U-boats.

The British did not have enough convoy escort ships, however, and large vessels proved ineffective at hunting U-boats. On September 7, 1939, the aircraft carrier HMS *Courageous* was torpedoed while it was on patrol. Worse was to follow. On October 14, the

Royal Navy was shaken when *U-47* sank HMS *Royal Oak*. It was not the loss of an old battleship that caused concern; rather it was the fact that the U-boat had penetrated Scapa Flow, the Royal Navy's main base in the Orkney Islands, north of Scotland.

Battle of the Plate River

Unlike the U-boats, the German surface ships were making few gains, although the pocket battleship *Admiral Graf Spee* sank 11 merchant ships in the South Atlantic and southern Indian Ocean between September and early December. The British gathered large forces to hunt the pocket battleship down.

On December 13, the *Graf Spee* was engaged by three British cruisers in the Battle of the Plate River off Montevideo, in neutral Uruguay. They were outgunned and all three warships were damaged, but they hit the *Graf Spee* hard enough to force it to withdraw into Montevideo harbor.

Under international law, the ship had just 72 hours in the harbor to make repairs before it had to sail or be seized. Captain Hans Langsdorff knew he would

be unable to complete repairs in time and was fooled into believing that he faced an overwhelming force of British warships. He scuttled (deliberately sank) the ship outside off the harbor and then committed suicide.

Britain holds its own

Germany's other surface raiders were not faring much better. In the North Atlantic the pocket battleship

---

Eyewitness Report:

❝ The mission seemed to be going well; boats were alongside and men were climbing up the rope ladders to safety. Suddenly, you could see the torpedo's trail as it knifed through the water toward the helpless *Patroclus*. We ducked behind the gun's shield to avoid shrapnel. A massive explosion rocked the ship when the torpedo struck ... and knocked us off our feet. Quickly getting back up, I looked down the side of the ship. What I saw can only be described as carnage, the men trying to reach safety having been exposed to the blast. The *Patroclus* began to list, but the U-boat continued to fire more torpedoes into the doomed ship. ❞

George Clarke, a Canadian serving on HMS *Patroclus* in a convoy off the coast of Ireland, November 1940

POCKET BATTLESHIPS

A painting of the Admiral Graf Spee during the Battle of the Plate River, off the coast of Uruguay, in December 1939.

Pocket battleships were designed as fast, heavily armed commerce raiders that could overtake and sink merchant ships, outgun enemy cruisers, and outrun enemy battleships. Known as *Panzerschiff* ("armored ships") in German, they were called pocket battleships in English because they were one-third of the size of full-size battleships. Germany planned to build six but only built three: *Deutschland*, later renamed *Lützow* (1931), *Admiral Scheer* (1933), and *Admiral Graf Spee* (1934).

The pocket battleships caused a sensation, but they were not as invincible as first thought. By 1939, other battleships had got quicker, and cruiser tactics had improved to deal with the new vessels. None of the pocket battleships had a particularly successful career.

Deutschland had to return home with engine trouble. The battle cruisers *Scharnhorst* and *Gneisenau* sank several merchant ships, but then fled for home rather than engage British naval units.

At the end of 1939 the British were holding their own in the Atlantic. The first wave of German surface raiders had tied up large numbers of warships but had actually sunk few merchant vessels. About 80 Allied or neutral ships had been sunk by mines and 114 by the U-boats, but such losses were manageable. More than 5500 vessels sailing in convoy had arrived safely, and nine enemy submarines had been sunk.

Crewmen on a German cruiser watch a merchant ship sink after they have attacked it.

By the end of 1940, however, Britain seemed to be close to losing the Battle of the Atlantic.

The Kreigsmarine advance

Germany gained a great advantage following the surrender of Norway and France in June 1940. The occupation of these countries gave the Kriegsmarine bases on the Atlantic that increased the reach of the U-boats and made it easier for long-range aircraft to locate targets. U-boats began to operate in the eastern Atlantic, patrolling the shipping routes to West and South Africa, and entering the Mediterranean to assist Italian forces.

The British, meanwhile, faced a shortage of ships. They were given 50 old destroyers by the United States in September, but from June 1940 they were forced to take warships off escort duty to combat Hitler's planned invasion of England. Escorts now only accompanied convoys up to 200 miles (320 km) west of Ireland. Although this had crept up to around 400 miles (640 km) by the end of 1939, the newer, longer-range U-boats usually hunted up to 700 miles (1,120 km) out in the Atlantic. There, they could operate largely unopposed.

U-BOAT TACTICS

In the early part of the war, the few German U-boats usually hunted alone, attacking targets in daylight when submerged. They only attacked on the surface with their deck guns against an unescorted merchant ship. As more U-boats were built, they continued to sail alone looking for prey. Once a convoy was sighted, however, the submarine tailed it while passing details of the location to other submarines. Once gathered in a "wolf pack" of around 15 to 20, the U-boats attacked together at night from all directions, surfacing to cruise up and down the columns of ships in the convoy.

Die Rudeltaktik (the wolf tactic), devised by Karl Dönitz, began in the fall of 1940 and was highly successful until 1943. Britain's initial lack of escorts made it a safe option, particularly as many escorts were slower than surfaced U-boats and lacked sonar to pinpoint U-boats underwater. Later in the war, faster escorts, better sonar equipment, and naval air power doomed the wolf packs to defeat.

A U-boat sails close to the English coast in 1940. Submarines would spend long periods of time on the surface, but would submerge when they wanted to attack targets during daylight.

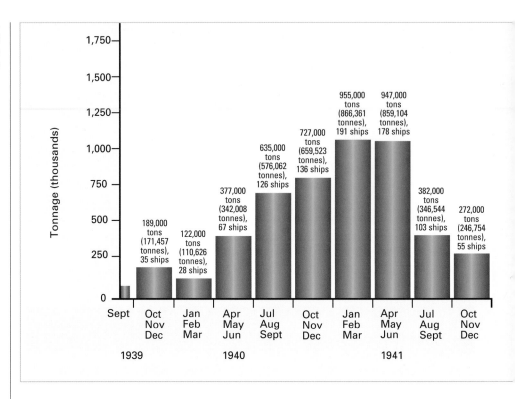

This chart shows Allied shipping losses in the Battle of the Atlantic during 1939–41.

Tonnage (thousands)

189,000 tons (171,457 tonnes), 35 ships

122,000 tons (110,626 tonnes), 28 ships

377,000 tons (342,008 tonnes), 67 ships

635,000 tons (576,062 tonnes), 126 ships

727,000 tons (659,523 tonnes), 136 ships

955,000 tons (866,361 tonnes), 191 ships

947,000 tons (859,104 tonnes), 178 ships

382,000 tons (346,544 tonnes), 103 ships

272,000 tons (246,754 tonnes), 55 ships

Sept | Oct Nov Dec | Jan Feb Mar | Apr May Jun | Jul Aug Sept | Oct Nov Dec | Jan Feb Mar | Apr May Jun | Jul Aug Sept | Oct Nov Dec

1939 — 1940 — 1941

Technicians on a German U-boat ready torpedoes for firing, in 1941.

Although probably no more than 16 U-boats were operating in the North Atlantic at any one time, they sank 3 million tons (2.7 million metric tons) of shipping in the second half of 1940. The German submariners called this the "Happy Time." Successful commanders became Nazi heroes.

By December 1940, the British had lost 20 percent of their prewar merchant fleet and had to build replacements fast enough to offset the losses. Equally worrying was the Royal Navy's inability to sink U-boats. During the "Happy Time," just six U-boats were lost.

The Royal Navy's failure was partly due to old anti-submarine equipment. Its depth charges (underwater bombs) and Asdic, an early form of sonar, were ineffective. Successful tactics for finding and destroying submarines also had to be mastered. In addition, the Royal Navy's support aircraft had only a limited range.

The wolf packs

With 20 U-boats being built each month, the scale of their operations grew rapidly. In 1941, U-boat captains extended their operations in the central

ENIGMA

In the late 1920s, the German military adopted a complex coding machine, a device that transformed a written message into rows of seemingly random numbers. The coded message was sent by radio and decoded by a similar machine at the receiving end. The British and French were given copies of the so-called Enigma machine by Polish decoders just before the war began. Code breaking remained extremely difficult, however, because the codes changed daily and there were several models of the machine. British code breakers were able to build a basic decoding machine known as Colossus early in the war that could read the enemy's transmissions after a time delay. The major breakthrough came in the Atlantic in March 1941, when a boarding party recovered a naval Enigma machine from *U-110*. The intelligence the British gathered, named *Ultra*, was vital to the Allied victory. The Germans did not know that their codes had been so thoroughly broken until after the war.

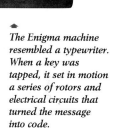

The Enigma machine resembled a typewriter. When a key was tapped, it set in motion a series of rotors and electrical circuits that turned the message into code.

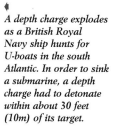

A depth charge explodes as a British Royal Navy ship hunts for U-boats in the south Atlantic. In order to sink a submarine, a depth charge had to detonate within about 30 feet (10m) of its target.

U.S. SINKINGS

Even before the United States entered World War II in December 1941, its merchant and naval ships were active in the Battle of the Atlantic, either acting as convoy escorts or taking supplies to Britain. US naval involvement increased in September 1941, when warships routinely began to protect convoys.

On October 17, the destroyer USS *Kearney* was torpedoed while attacking a U-boat, but limped home. The destroyer *Reuben James* became the first U.S. ship to fall victim to enemy fire when it was torpedoed by *U-562* west of Ireland on October 31. The deaths of 125 seamen in these attacks hardened U.S. feeling against Nazi Germany.

and western Atlantic, and Admiral Karl Dönitz, commander of the submarine force, developed a new tactic. If a U-boat spotted a convoy, it radioed its position to other U-boats in the area. When a so-called "wolf pack" of 15 to 20 U-boats had come together, they overwhelmed the escort vessels and attacked the convoy.

By the end of 1941, some 432 Allied ships had been sunk by submarines in the Atlantic, and operational U-boat numbers had increased fourfold. The number of sinkings was below that of

1940, however, and some 35 U-boats had been lost, while several of the top aces had been killed or captured.

The surface war

German surface raiders had mixed fortunes in 1940. In October, the pocket battleship *Admiral Scheer* slipped into the North Atlantic. On a four-month cruise in the South Atlantic and southern Indian Ocean, it destroyed 17 Allied vessels. However, the raid had not begun particularly well. On November 5, its captain spied a weakly escorted Allied convoy, but *Admiral Sheer*'s attack was met by HMAS *Jervis Bay*, an armed merchant cruiser. Although it was less well armed, the *Jervis Bay* kept the battleship at bay for an hour before being sunk: the delay allowed most of the convoy vessels to escape.

In 1941, Germany's surface raiders continued their efforts. On March 18, the *Scharnhorst* and *Gneisenau* met a convoy scattering from a U-boat attack. They sank 16 merchant ships in two days, before sailing to Brest on the French coast to escape British

The survivors of a sinking Allied ship row to a U-boat to be taken prisoner.

battleships. While at anchor both ships were bombed and put out of action for months. Meanwhile, the heavy cruiser *Admiral Hipper* made successful raids into the North Atlantic in February before returning to Germany in April.

Sinking the *Bismarck*

Germany's most powerful battleship was the *Bismarck*, which in May sailed with the heavy cruiser *Prinz Eugen* from Norway. They aimed to destroy merchant shipping in the Atlantic. Two days later, in the Battle of the Denmark Strait, north of Iceland, *Bismarck* sank the British battle cruiser HMS *Hood* and badly damaged the battleship *Prince of Wales*. *Bismarck* had suffered a ruptured fuel tank, however, and headed for Brest while the *Prinz Eugen* sailed into the Atlantic.

The British sent all available ships to hunt down the *Bismarck*. By the evening of May 24, four battleships, two battle cruisers, two aircraft carriers, twelve cruisers, and several destroyers were in pursuit of the German ship. On May 26, torpedoes from aircraft based on the carrier HMS *Ark Royal* struck *Bismarck*, flooding the steering room and leaving the ship circling aimlessly. The next day the British battleships *Rodney* and *King George V* closed in and left *Bismarck* a burning wreck. It was finally sunk by torpedoes. Only 110 of *Bismarck*'s 2200 crew survived.

Britain fights back

In the months following the loss of the *Bismarck*, British vessels sank or captured many of the supply vessels that supported Germany's warships. Meanwhile, the scale of Allied losses to submarines hid a deeper truth: the Allies were slowly discovering effective ways to defeat the German threat. The ever-present danger from mines was reduced, for example, as the Allies found more efficient ways

A victorious U-boat crew celebrate as they return to port from the Atlantic.

to remove them. More significantly, the first convoy was escorted by warships all the way across the Atlantic thanks to the gradual expansion of the Royal and Canadian navies.

The British had also developed better equipment, including a radar to detect targets on the surface, and starshells, which were artillery shells that released a shower of lights to illuminate targets at night. In September, they launched the first of a new type of small escort carrier, HMS *Audacity*, which was a merchant ship fitted with a flight deck to carry six fighter planes. The fighters could spot U-boats on the surface, and also fight off German long-range reconnaissance aircraft.

Audacity was sunk in December, but the concept of the small escort carrier was sound, and many more were built in 1942. Meanwhile long-range aircraft operating from Iceland, where Britain

13

GERMAN U-BOATS

The U-boat fleet of submarines was by far the most dangerous part of the German Navy.

U-boat is an anglicized version of the German word for submarine, *U-boot*—itself an abbreviation of *"Unterseeboot."* Although the terms of the Paris Peace Conference of 1919 forbade the construction of submarines, Germany managed to do some work on submarine development before Hitler came to power in 1933. After this date, the pace of building increased, and by 1939 there were 65 U-boats in service.

The speed and range of U-boats underwater were limited because, once submerged, they relied on battery power. This meant they spent most of their time on the surface, diving only when they were attacking by day or when they themselves were attacked by aircraft. Indeed, the most common U-boat attacks early in the war were surface attacks at night.

The backbone of the U-boat fleet was the Type VII, of which some 700 saw service. The U-boat with the longest range was the Type IX, some traveling as far as Japan and the east coast of the United States. The Type XIV was a large craft, used to resupply other U-boats at sea. The most advanced model, which did not come into service until late in the war, was the Type XXI. These boats boasted a streamlined hull design and a very large battery that gave them previously unheard of duration and speed underwater.

Added to the battery, the Type XXI U-boats had a *Schnorchel* (snorkel): a retractable pipe which supplied air to the diesel engines while submerged at periscope depth, allowing the boats to cruise and recharge their batteries while remaining unseen.

Above: **The German engineer Helmuth Walter developed a circuit motor that could function independently of oxygen from the atmosphere, using concentrated hydrogen peroxide. The Walter engine enabled U-boats to cruise at up to 28 knots underwater. The boat shown here is U-1405, one of just three completed vessels fitted with this revolutionary system. Had it been available earlier, the Walter system would have given U-boats a big advantage in the Battle of the Atlantic.**

Below right: U-81 *was a Type VIIC submarine. She began her career operating against the Arctic convoys in July 1941. However, she was redeployed to the Mediterranean in October that year, and in November achieved her greatest success when one of a salvo of four torpedoes that she fired hit the British aircraft carrier* Ark Royal. *The carrier sank the following day.*

Above: U-2501 *was a Type XXI "electro-boat" which had large spaces for batteries powering an electric motor that gave them 15 knots of speed underwater. They also had a snorkel, a faster reloading system for the bow torpedo tubes, and electronic detectors to warn that radar-carrying aircraft were above. It also carried twin 30mm anti-aircraft guns.*

Above: The conning tower of U-47, *a Type VIIB submarine. The Type VIIB was a slightly larger version of the Type VIIA. U-47 achieved fame early in the war when her commander, Gunther Prien, led her through the defenses of the major Royal Navy base of Scapa Flow and sank the battleship* Royal Oak.

Left: U-106, *a Type IXB long-range U-boat. The Type B craft had extra fuel tanks which gave them a range of 10,062 miles (16,100km) of surface cruising. U-106 was deployed in the Atlantic, and she enjoyed much success in the first six months of 1941. On the night of March 19/20, she torpedoed the battleship* Malaya, *which was on convoy escort duty; although she did not sink,* Malaya *never saw active service again.*

had had bases since May 1940, were also forcing U-boats to operate farther out in the Atlantic. Allied shipping losses fell dramatically in the final three months of 1941. This was partly because Hitler insisted that Dönitz send more than 25 U-boats into the Mediterranean, but was equally a result of growing skill at anti-submarine operations.

Help from the United States

Such improvements were important, but it was the involvement of the United States that really gave Britain renewed hope during 1941. In March, the U.S. government introduced the Lend-Lease Act, which gave President Roosevelt the power to "lend" war equipment to countries whose defense was vital to U.S. interests. Britain soon placed orders for escorts and long-range patrol aircraft.

In April, Roosevelt announced that Greenland, a distant part of Nazi-occupied Denmark, was to be made a U.S. protectorate to prevent it being used as an Axis base. In July, the first U.S. troops arrived in Iceland to take over bases used by the British.

Roosevelt met Churchill in Newfoundland, Canada, in August and agreed that U.S. warships would escort convoys west of Greenland. The U.S. convoys began on September 16, allowing the British to intensify their anti-submarine operations with warships freed from escort duty.

A new phase

On December 11, four days after the Japanese attack on the U.S. base at Pearl Harbor, Germany declared war on the United States. On December 22, Churchill and Roosevelt met at the Arcadia Conference in Washington and agreed that the Allies' priority was to defeat Germany and Italy. The Battle of the Atlantic was about to enter its decisive stage.

CHAPTER 2
THE WAR ON THE ARCTIC CONVOYS

British and American aid to the Soviet Union was channeled across the Arctic Sea, but the hazards were enormous for the cargo ships involved, as German aircraft, submarines, and ships based in Norway pounced on the Allied convoys.

Grand Admiral Erich Raeder, commander of the German Kriegsmarine. He planned to use U-boats and surface ships to destroy Allied convoys in the Atlantic Ocean.

Previous pages: A merchantman of PQ17 goes down after being hit by a U-boat torpedo. This photograph was taken by the attacking U-boat.

The Norwegian campaign of 1940 was a brilliant tactical success for the Germans, in which initial surprise and air superiority had counterbalanced the importance of British sea power. The invasion had been launched for strategic naval reasons, but the significance and benefits of the operation were tempered by the losses suffered by the Kriegsmarine (German Navy).

Germany had gained naval and air bases in Norway ideal for launching raids on British maritime communications, and made the imposition of a naval blockade on Germany more difficult. Yet the losses to the Kriegsmarine meant that its surface strength was effectively crippled for the rest of war, undermining its potential to exploit fully the strategic advantages accrued from the possession of Norway. Meanwhile, the British quietly occupied Iceland, which somewhat lessened the benefits that the Germans had gained by making the route to the Atlantic by the northern passages more difficult.

Raeder's plans

By the autumn of 1940, the Royal Navy was increasingly stretched. The French defeat and the entry of Italy into the war threatened British control of the Mediterranean, while the Japanese were becoming increasingly aggressive in East Asia. Nonetheless, the German Navy remained the main threat. Grand Admiral Erich Raeder, the Commander-in-Chief of the Kriegsmarine, hoped to disperse the Royal Navy's superior strength and, with the aid of his U-boat fleet, to attack and cut Great Britain's vital Atlantic supply lines. The U-boats would force the Royal Navy to concentrate shipping in convoys, and surface ships would then destroy these convoys. The pocket battleship *Admiral Scheer* broke into the Atlantic in October 1940 and sunk 99,000 tons (100,584 metric tonnes) of Allied shipping during her five-month cruise. She was followed

One of Raeder's U-boats. German submarines tended to gather around convoys like wolves around a flock of sheep, waiting for any stray to become separated from the flock.

by the *Admiral Hipper*, now repaired after clashing with *Glowworm*. The battle cruisers *Scharnhorst* and *Gneisenau* sank or captured 22 merchantmen, totaling nearly 116,000 tons (117,856 metric tonnes), between January and March 1941. That March losses in the Atlantic to surface raiders, U-boats, and aircraft were the severest yet, totaling over 350,000 tons (355,600 metric tonnes). Raeder's strategy appeared to be working.

Furthermore, two large 50,000-ton (50,800-metric-tonne) battleships, *Bismarck* and *Tirpitz*, were nearing completion. Given the strategic situation, the only task Raeder could give the *Bismarck* was raiding in the Atlantic. He intended to send her out with the heavy cruiser *Prinz Eugen*, and make a simultaneous sortie with the *Scharnhorst* and *Gneisenau* from Brest. British bombing of the *Gneisenau* and the fact that the refit of the *Scharnhorst* would take longer than expected

scuppered this plan, but Raeder still sent out the *Bismarck* and *Prinz Eugen* on May 18, 1941. The ships were spotted by the Swedish Navy, and the pro-British Major Törnberg of the Swedish Intelligence Service passed the information to the military attaché of the Norwegian Government-in-Exile, Colonel Captain Roscher Lund. This

The German battleship Bismarck *photographed from the deck of the cruiser* Prinz Eugen.

Admiral Karl Dönitz speaks to some of his U-boat crews.

The Admiral Scheer fires a salvo at an Allied merchantman. In 1940, the Scheer sank thousands of tons of Allied shipping.

Winston Churchill immediately offered British aid and pledged to supply the Soviets as far as possible. This meant sending convoys on a 2,000-mile (3,200-km) journey via Norway's North Cape to Russia's only ice-free Arctic port, Murmansk. The first convoy, codenamed Dervish, sailed on August 21, carrying aircraft for the defense of Murmansk. It arrived safely. On September 29, the first of the regular convoys codenamed "PQ" sailed (the return journey was codenamed "QP"). By the end of the year, eight convoys had arrived safely, a total of 55 merchant vessels.

The Royal Navy also began operating more aggressively in the Arctic. There were sound strategic reasons for this. Due to the poor transport infrastructure in northern Norway and Finland, the Germans were supplying the forces that were attacking Murmansk by sea. Indeed, during 1942 nearly 6 million tons (6,096,000 metric tonnes) of materiel were convoyed around the North Cape to Petsamo. General Dietl's Arctic campaign was almost entirely reliant on these seaborne supplies. On July 30, 1941, the British launched two costly carrier-borne air attacks on the heavily defended ports of Kirkenes and Petsamo. In August, they mounted a raid against Spitsbergen and, in December, more spectacularly, two commando raids were launched against the Lofotens and Vagsoy. All this added to Hitler's fears that the British were preparing an invasion of Norway. However, the Germans did not seriously attempt to interfere with the convoys until early 1942, by which time their forces in Norway had increased dramatically.

started the chain of events which led to the encounter between the German ships and HMS *Hood* and HMS *Prince of Wales*. Although the *Hood* was destroyed in the clash, the *Bismarck* was damaged and subsequently sunk in the Atlantic, with important repercussions on German naval strategy.

In an effort to disrupt the iron-ore traffic, damage the Norwegian fish-oil industry, and give the newly formed commandos some experience, on March 4, 1941, the Royal Navy landed 500 commandos at four fishing ports on the Lofoten Islands. They caused considerable damage, sinking 18,000 tons (18,288 metric tonnes) of shipping and capturing codewheels and books for the German Enigma machine.

The whole war changed after the German invasion of the Soviet Union on June 22, 1941. British Prime Minister

Shifts in German strategy

Three events—the sinking of the *Bismarck*, the commando raids on Norway, and a realization in Berlin that

Eyewitness Report:

"The snow and the sleet squalls passed. Wednesday gave a clear cerulean sky, a blue and gleaming sea, very little horizon or zenith cloud. This was their day, the Nazis', we knew. We dragged our ammunition cases closer to the guns; got ready as well as we could.

They came early: the Heinkels, the Messerschmitts, the Stukas, the Junkers 89's, and all told there were 105 of them over us during that day's fight that was to last twenty hours. They used everything: 1100-pounders, 550's, 250's, aerial torpedoes, mines, their cannons, and their machine guns; while outside, always trying to get in, their submarines rushed our escort.

That was hell. There is no other word I know for it. Everywhere you looked aloft you saw them, crossing and recrossing us, hammering down and back, the bombs brown, sleek in the air, screaming to burst furiously white in the sea. All around us, as so slowly we kept on going, the pure blue of the sea was mottled blackish with the greasy patches of their bomb discharges. Our ship was missed closely time and again. We drew our breaths in a kind of gasping-choke.

At about half-past ten that morning, the long-shanked Fourth Mate and I were on the after guns on the poop. Two Messerschmitts came after us, off the bank of broken cloud on the northern horizon. Since Monday, the Messerschmitt squadrons had given our ship a lot of attention, no doubt remembering their pal we had nailed. This pair came down in one-two formation, the aftermost perhaps three hundred feet (91 meters) behind his partner. At the start of their dive on us they had about two thousand foot (610 meters) altitude.

It was my first time to fire at them, and, eager and excited, I shot too soon. My tracers curved off; I was out of range, so I cut the guns. But they kept on coming, bigger and bigger in the ring sights, their wings growing from thin lines to thick fierceness from which lanced gun flame. We could see the bombs in the racks; we could see the bombardiers. Together, the Fourth Mate and I cut in at them.

We were leaning far back, knees bent, hands hard on the rubber grips, fingers down on the triggers, eyes to the ring sights. We were no longer conscious of the empties clacketing out underfoot, of the cold, the trembling motion of the ship as the other bombs burst. Here was death, and we were throwing death back to meet it.

The aftermost plane peeled off, banking toward the ship astern. The other kept on, right into our fire, smack for us. Then he dropped it, a 550-pounder. He was gone, away from our fire, and, hanging to the guns, all we could do was look up at that bomb.

Then in some sudden and not-yet-strong gust of wind it veered a bit. It struck the sea no more than twenty-five feet (7.5 meters) astern of us. There was the impact of passage into the sea, an immense, rushing smack, then the detonation. My wife's image was before my eyes. I stood there waiting for the T.N.T.

Water went tumbling over me in a dousing, blinding column. The ship rose and fell, groaning, terribly shaking. Empty cartridges jumped under the shock, pitched off into the sea. Beneath my feet, as the ship still jarred from that awful violence, the deck seams opened, and the oakum lay loose.

Water dripped from my helmet brim into my eyes. I was soaked from the collar of my sheepskin coat to my felt-lined boots. Beside me, still at his station between me and the Fourth Mate's guns, was old Ben. He was the oldest A.B. in the ship; Ben, a Baltimore man, who in the last war had seen service at the front in France. He might have run as that bomb fell, taken out forward for the life boats on the boat deck, anywhere away from the bomb. But he stayed there; he just bent his knees and set himself and waited, empty-handed and where he belonged."

Robert Carse, a seaman aboard the SS *Steel Worker* as it made its way along the Norwegian coast

Soviet destroyers sail out of Murmansk on their way to meet an Allied convoy in 1941. The Germans attempted to intercept Soviet warships before they linked up with the convoys.

The Bismarck *fires at HMS* Hood *during her last battle in May 1941. The loss of the* Bismarck *was a major loss for the Kriegsmarine.*

the Arctic convoys were important— all had major effects on German naval strategy. After the loss of the *Bismarck*, the German naval staff did not give up the idea of further surface operations in the Atlantic, and had planned to send the *Tirpitz* out with the *Hipper*. In November 1941, Hitler decided to send the *Tirpitz* to Trondheim rather than into the Atlantic. He ordered a heavy reinforcement of land and air forces and demanded that "every available vessel be employed in Norway."

This was a major shift in German policy and it was further reinforced by Hitler's decision that the *Scharnhorst* and *Gneisenau*, based at Brest, should join the *Tirpitz* in Norway. In an audacious operation in February 1942, the two battle cruisers, together with the heavy cruiser *Prinz Eugen*, returned to German waters via the English Channel, causing considerable embarrassment to the Royal Navy and the RAF. Only the *Scharnhorst* could join the *Tirpitz* in Norway seven months later. Despite the blow to British pride, this tactical victory was essentially a strategic withdrawal.

By early 1942 German naval units in Norway consisted of the *Tirpitz*, the pocket battleships *Lützow* and *Admiral Scheer*, the heavy cruisers *Prinz Eugen* and *Hipper*, the light cruiser *Köln*, five destroyers, and 20 U-boats. The main concern of the British was that the German ships in Norway, particularly the *Tirpitz*, did not break out into the Atlantic. Just after she arrived in Norwegian waters, Winston Churchill described the destruction of the warship as "the greatest event at sea at the present time. No other target is comparable to it." He asserted that "the

The British assigned aircraft carriers as convoy escorts. These ships are HMS Biter *(left) and* Avenger *(right). The aircraft on the* Avenger *are Hurricanes. Note the heavy seas that were a feature of the Arctic convoy routes.*

whole strategy of the war turns at this period on this ship which is holding four times the number of British capital ships paralyzed, to say nothing of the two new American battleships retained in the Atlantic." As a result, the first British bombing missions were launched against the *Tirpitz* in late January 1942.

Tirpitz made a sortie against British convoys early in March. On March 8, appalling weather prevented aerial reconnaissance on both sides, and on that day two convoys, the British Home Fleet, and the *Tirpitz* were all within 80 miles (130 km) of each other. Admiral Ciliax, German C-in-C Battleships, decided to turn for home. Tovey, aided by Ultra intercepts of German naval traffic, was able to set off in pursuit and launch an air strike from *Victorious* on March 9. The *Tirpitz* put up a tremendous anti-aircraft barrage against the determined but inexperienced air crews. Two British aircraft were lost and the German ship was able to put safely into Narvik. The close escape caused Raeder to place further restrictions on German surface operations. There were to be no sorties until air reconnaissance

had fully determined the strength of the enemy.

Nonetheless, on March 14, 1942, Hitler decided to make the Arctic convoys a strategic target of major importance linked directly to the campaign in Russia, as the Anglo-American deliveries of war supplies were "sustaining Russian ability to hold out." Apart from the *Tirpitz*'s ineffectual sortie, the only loss suffered by the Arctic convoys was a 5,135-ton (5,217-metric-tonne) merchantman from PQ7, sunk by Lieutenant Rudolf Schend's *U-134*. But with Hitler's intervention this was about to change. Quite apart from the formidable German surface and submarine units based in Norway, two specialized Luftwaffe anti-shipping units, KG 26 and KG 30, were transferred to the air bases at Bardufoss and Banak.

There were, however, serious limitations placed on naval operations by the critical nature of the German fuel-oil shortage. The loss of Soviet oil due to the launching of Barbarossa added impetus to the German drive toward the Caucasian oilfields. The Ploesti oilfields

> "There were serious limitations placed on naval operations by the critical nature of the German fuel oil shortage"

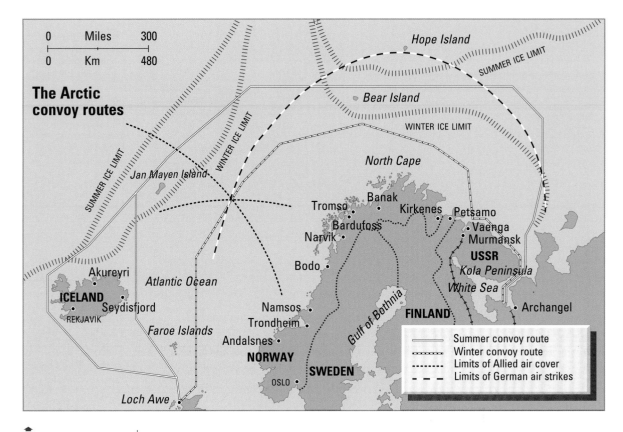

The Arctic convoy routes

0   Miles   300
0   Km   480

Hope Island

SUMMER ICE LIMIT

Bear Island

WINTER ICE LIMIT

North Cape

Banak

Tromso   Kirkenes   Petsamo

Bardufoss   Vaenga

Narvik   Murmansk

Jan Mayen Island

SUMMER ICE LIMIT

WINTER ICE LIMIT

Bodo

USSR

Akureyri   Atlantic Ocean   Kola Peninsula

ICELAND   White Sea

Seydisfjord

REKJAVIK   Namsos   FINLAND   Archangel

Faroe Islands   Trondheim

Andalsnes   Gulf of Bothnia

NORWAY

SWEDEN

OSLO

Loch Awe

	Summer convoy route
	Winter convoy route
	Limits of Allied air cover
	Limits of German air strikes

This map illustrates the vulnerability of the Arctic convoys to air and sea attacks. In summer, the risks to the convoys were reduced but not eradicated.

in Romania were the only Axis source of petroleum and also fueled the Italian fleet, which was dependent on them. Therefore, just as Hitler demanded an increase in surface attacks on the convoys, the German Naval Command had to order that: "All operations are to be discontinued, including those by light forces." The Kriegsmarine received only a tenth of its monthly fuel requirement that April. The U-boats were unaffected as they used diesel oil. But from about February 1942 onward, all surface operations were governed by the availability of fuel.

Despite these problems, German pressure on the convoys was increasing, although it was largely U-boats and aircraft that were doing the damage. PQ13 endured both terrible weather and constant German attack. It was spotted by a BV 138B flying-boat on March 28. Ju 88s of III/KG 30 sank two stragglers.

In what was described as a "miracle," Rear-Admiral Hubert Schmundt, Flag Officer Northern Waters—or "Admiral Arctic"—was given specific permission to send out three destroyers from Kirkenes after the convoy: Z24, Z25, and Z26, under Captain Pönitz. After picking up a number of survivors from the air attacks, he gained enough intelligence to enable Fritz von Berger's Z26 to sink a stray freighter on March 29. Z26's luck did not hold as it encountered the British cruiser HMS Trinidad and came under accurate gunfire. Z26's fate would have been sealed had one of Trinidad's torpedoes not malfunctioned and returned to hit the British ship. Z26 escaped, only to tangle with the British destroyer Eclipse, which inflicted further damage before being driven off by Z26's sister ships. The German destroyers did not pursue but took off Z26's crew before the ship slowly sank. PQ13's ordeal was not yet over,

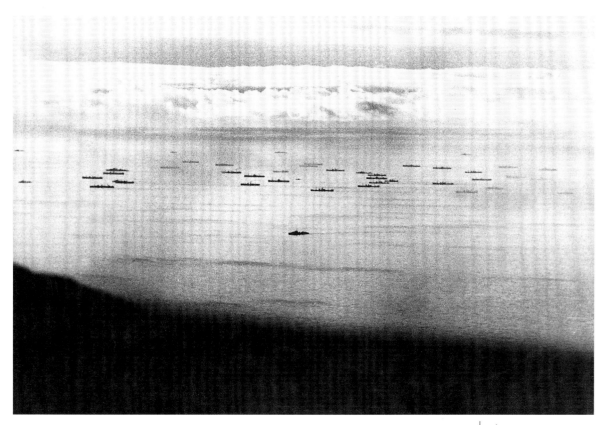

as *U-376* and *U-435* both sank a further merchantman each. Nineteen ships had set out with PQ13 and five had been lost.

PQ14 fared somewhat better. Although attacked by the Luftwaffe on April 15, no ships were hit. The submariners were more successful, and Captain Lieutenant Heinz-Ehlert in *U-403* torpedoed a merchant ship on April 16. This was the convoy's only loss. By now, there were 20 U-boats operating in the Arctic, and Grand Admiral Dönitz transferred them to Schmundt's control.

The assault on PQ15

The German effort continued. PQ15, made up of 25 merchantmen with a strong destroyer escort, was spotted by the Luftwaffe on April 30, 250 miles (400 km) southwest of Bear Island. The first air attacks did not occur until March 2, but these were "raggedly and poorly executed." The convoy remained

under continued surveillance by aircraft and U-boats. In the early hours of May 3, six aircraft from I/KG 26 attacked and managed to sink three ships. *Trinidad* had to be scuttled after further bomb damage. Another cruiser, HMS *Edinburgh*, escorting QP11, was hit by two torpedoes from Captain Lieutenant Max Martin Teichert's *U-456* on April

The ill-fated convoy PQ17. This photograph was taken by a German reconnaissance aircraft during the early stages of the convoy's journey to Murmansk.

Keeping watch for the enemy as PQ17 makes its way north.

Eyewitness Report:

As Chief Steward of the *Empire Tide* of the Royal Mail Line, in convoy PQ.17 for Archangel in 1942 (one of the few ships to survive), Horace Carswell mixed other excitements with the suddenly assumed role of surgeon.

" Our convoy altered course and steamed due east through a sea a-glitter with floe-ice. Not long afterward we reached a position near Bear Island, the zone of greatest danger, lying within easy range of the German airbases. The alarm bells were soon ringing for 'Action Stations.'

Between forty and fifty Jerries came racing in from all directions... that filled the Arctic sky with the thunder of high-powered engines. It was the Fourth of July. A ship on the *Empire Tide*'s port quarter erupted like a volcano and disappeared... Two or three others began to lose way, then listed and settled deeply from the impacts of bombs and the deadly 'fish.'

Fragments of ice from the shattered floes spattered our decks. Warships and merchantmen combined to fill the sky with the fury of high-explosives, and the rain of steel made you thankful for a tin 'battle bowler,' inadequate protection though it was.

For handling and fighting his ship that day, Captain Frank Willis Harvey, master of the *Empire Tide*, was awarded the DSO... **"**

Chief Engineer Hughes and Second Engineer Griffith remained in the engine-room, ensuring the utmost possible speed under conditions of great stress

The Focke-Wulf Fw 200 Kondor was a long-range reconnaissance and attack aircraft. It was nicknamed the "Scourge of the Atlantic," although the Luftwaffe never had enough of them to have a decisive impact on the Arctic convoys to and from Russia.

30. Although the *Edinburgh*'s destroyers prevented Teichert from finishing the ship off, he maintained contact, and this prompted Schmundt to send out three destroyers, Z24, Z25, and the *Hermann Schoemann*. They made contact with the convoy on May 1 and made five attempts to attack it, but the aggressive tactics of the escorting destroyers kept them at bay, although a German torpedo sank a Soviet merchantman.

That evening Captain Alfred Schulze-Hinrichs, commanding the operation, decided to go after the *Edinburgh*. The British escorts did their best to keep the German ships at a distance, and a 6-in salvo from *Edinburgh* hit the *Hermann Schoemann*. Z24, however, managed a torpedo hit on *Edinburgh*, and Rear-Admiral Bonham-Carter ordered that the ship be abandoned.

The steady growth of losses, particularly the two cruisers, led Admiral Bonham-Carter to comment: "Until the aerodromes in north Norway are neutralized and there are some hours of darkness, the continuation of these convoys should be stopped. If they must continue for political reasons, very serious and heavy losses must be expected. The force of German attacks will increase, not diminish."

Tovey agreed and wanted the convoys kept small. The British Chief of Staff (COS) committee also had doubts about the wisdom of continuing the policy. However, Churchill insisted that the convoys continue, claiming that the United States and the Soviets both expected the British to maintain their effort: "Failure on our part to make the attempt would weaken our influence with both our major Allies... I share your misgivings but I feel that it is a matter of duty."

The German light cruiser Köln was one of the ships earmarked to attack PQ18, but was not used due to Hitler's fear of naval losses.

So PQ16, of 35 merchantmen—the biggest convoy so far—sailed from Rekjavik on May 21, 1942. On May 27, more than 100 aircraft attacked over a 10-hour period and succeeded in sinking six ships and damaging many more. Although there were a couple more half-hearted attacks over the following days, the worst was over. Despite the losses, Tovey believed that the "convoy's success was beyond expectation."

The British were proving capable of dealing with the U-boat and Luftwaffe threat, but the German heavy ships were another matter. It was inexplicable that they had not attacked seriously—the British were not aware of German fuel shortages—and the Admiralty knew that there was no defense against them. British capital ships could not enter the Barents Sea until they were sure that the *Tirpitz* was not making for the Atlantic. In any case the Barents Sea, filled with U-boats and in range of German land-based bombers, was too dangerous a place. Essentially, the British believed they had no real defense against the *Tirpitz* if she caught a convoy east of Bear Island. All that could be done was to order the convoy to scatter.

Unfortunately for the British, the Germans had decided to attack the next convoy in strength using the *Tirpitz*, *Hipper*, and the two pocket battleships based in Norway. When Raeder proposed targeting PQ17 on June 15, Hitler expressed grave concern about the operation, codenamed *Rösselsprung* (Knight's Move). Fearing the threat of British carrier-borne aircraft he ordered that, "the aircraft carriers must be located before the attack, and they must be rendered harmless by our Ju 88 planes before the attack gets under way." Once more the Führer had placed serious limitations on his naval officers' freedom of action. Even so, Raeder transferred his heavy ships north, although the *Lützow* and three destroyers ran aground outside Narvik.

> "The Barents Sea, filled with U-boats and in range of German land-based bombers, was too dangerous a place"

Although very advanced at the time of its design (1933), the Russian Polikarpov I-16 was obsolete by 1942. However, as more than 7000 were produced, it was an important machine. Modern aircraft were used on the main fronts, and older types, such as the I-16, were relegated to the Arctic Front.

The other ships reached the anchorage at Altenfjord without incident.

RAF reconnaissance showed that their berths at Trondheim were empty, and Enigma decrypts indicated that the *Tirpitz* was preparing to put to sea. Dudley Pound, the British Chief of the Naval Staff, was well aware of the catastrophe that would occur if the *Tirpitz*, *Hipper*, *Scheer*, and, for all he knew, *Lützow* as well caught the convoy. He ordered the escort withdrawn and the convoy to scatter. The *Tirpitz* had made her most destructive contribution to the naval war without firing her guns. By her

threatened presence, she had broken up a convoy, something all the U-boats and aircraft in northern Norway had failed to do. When it was clear that the convoy had scattered, she turned back to Altenfjord, leaving the slaughter to aircraft and U-boats. Twenty-four ships were lost over the following days, and only 12 made it to Murmansk.

German morale problems

Nonetheless, there were problems of morale amongst the men of the German surface fleet in Norway. They were hampered by their increasingly restrictive orders and had seen virtually no action. The German heavy ships had been sitting in their Arctic berths for months, enduring occasional British air attack. The climate, particularly in winter, is extremely harsh and the Norwegian ports offered very limited diversions for off-duty sailors. Boredom is not good for morale and the officers were well aware of the problem.

The British Admiralty demanded that the Arctic convoys cease through the summer months, and so PQ18 did not sail until September. Forty merchant

Another aircraft used on the Arctic Front against German shipping was the Russian Tupolev SB–2. The camouflage scheme is an interesting one, swirls of color with few, if any, markings. The capacity was 1,325 lbs (600 kg) of bombs stowed internally.

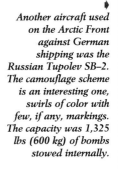

ships were assembled, and for the first time an Arctic convoy was given its own local air cover by the inclusion of the escort carrier HMS *Avenger*. An anti-aircraft cruiser, HMS *Scylla*, 16 destroyers, and a whole host of corvettes, trawlers, and minesweepers completed the convoy's protection. The Home Fleet would provide distant cover. The Germans had also made considerable plans for PQ18, boosted by their success against the previous convoy. The *Scheer*, *Hipper*, and the light cruiser *Köln* were moved to Altenfjord. Hitler, as ever, insisted they take no risks, so Raeder canceled the operation. The Germans had assembled a considerable force in northern Norway. Forty-two He 111H-6 torpedo bombers of KG 26 were joined by 35 Junkers Ju 88A-17s, a new Ju 88 modification also capable of carrying torpedoes, flown in specially from France. They would operate in combination with the Ju 88 bombers of

KG 30 using a tactic called the *Goldern Zange* (Golden Comb). Mid-level and dive-bombing by KG 30 would break up the cohesion of the British escorts, while low-level torpedo attacks would do the real damage. Göring told his pilots that a victory over PQ18 would be of vital significance to the war against the Soviet Union, as it would deprive the Red Army of important equipment and thus ease the progress of the army at Stalingrad and the drive into the Caucasus.

On September 13, 20 Ju 88s of KG 30 carried out a high-level diversionary run, which caused the required degree of disruption. They were followed by the torpedo bombers of KG 26, 28 He 111s in two waves, followed by 18 Ju 88s from Bardufoss. Another 17 Ju 88s of KG 30 from Banak were in support. The convoy opened up with everything it had; the Germans came in so low that even the 4.7-in guns of the destroyers could be brought into action.

A Soviet light anti-aircraft gun waits for a clear sighting outside of Murmansk. The soldier to the left of the gun is using a range finder to determine the distance to the target.

They pressed their attacks with suicidal daring and flew in among the ships, dropping their torpedoes at very close range. Eight ships were lost in a matter of minutes, at the cost of only five aircraft.

The next air attack, by Heinkel He 115 seaplanes of the Kriegsmarine flying out of Billefjord, was a much more half-hearted affair. They lost two aircraft and were driven off, at the cost of one Hurricane. On the 14th, *U-457* sank the tanker *Athel Templar* and escaped the pursuing destroyers by diving under the convoy and becoming lost amid the noise of the convoy's propellers. The losses were not all one way: HMS *Onslow* destroyed *U-589*. A specific attack by Ju 88s of KG 26 was made on HMS *Avenger* that day and was broken up with the loss of 11 aircraft. Dive-

bombing by KG 30 continued, and in the afternoon another attempt was made on the aircraft carrier, but this also failed to sink her. Five bombers were lost and nine so badly damaged that they were later declared unserviceable.

In all, 13 merchant ships out of 40 had been sunk, 10 by aircraft and three by U-boats. However, the Germans had lost 41 aircraft and three submarines. The loss of such highly trained crews was a serious blow. So PQ18 was an Allied victory, albeit a very expensive one. It also marked a turning point in the Arctic naval war, as the Germans would never again be able to muster such numbers of aircraft in the area. Luftflotte 5 was stripped in the wake of the Allied landings in North Africa. When the next convoy sailed for Russia, Luftwaffe resources in northern

Norway were limited to long-range reconnaissance aircraft and He 115s.

After PQ18, convoys had been suspended due to the demands of the invasion of North Africa on the Home Fleet. However, the Admiralty decided to restart them by sending JW51 in two parts in mid-December.

The Battle of the Barents Sea

In Germany, Hitler remained obsessed with the possibility of an Allied landing in Norway. He sent the now-repaired *Lützow* back, adding to the very strong German naval presence there. On December 30, 1942, when a U-boat reported the British convoy JW51B south of Bear Island, Raeder took advantage of this strength by authorizing the *Hipper* and *Lützow* to intercept the convoy. Operation *Regenbogen* (Rainbow) was intended by its commander, Vice-Admiral Oskar Kummetz, to catch JW51B in a pincer between the *Hipper* and *Lützow*.

Contact was made on December 31. The skillful use of the British destroyer escort forced Kummetz, aboard the vastly superior *Hipper*, away from the convoy. However, his plan was working: The convoy turned toward the south and was now without escort, as this had been committed against the *Hipper*. JW51B was at the *Lützow*'s mercy. Meanwhile, two British cruisers began to engage the *Hipper*, and Kummetz, mindful of his instructions,

During the early years of the war, Great Britain supplied hundreds of aircraft to the USSR via the Arctic ports. Here, a Hurricane fighter is being loaded for transport to points south.

An alternative use of the PTRD 14.5mm anti-tank rifle was as an anti-aircraft gun. This single shot weapon could, in the hands of a crack-shot, deliver a fatal blow to slow, lightly protected reconnaissance aircraft. This gun was part of the Soviet defenses around Murmansk.

THE SINKING OF THE *SCHARNHORST*

The reduction in German forces and the return of the British Home Fleet to something like full strength after the invasion of Sicily in July 1943 enabled the British to take a more offensive stance off the coast of Norway, and also to restart the convoys. A carrier-launched air attack took place against the port of Bodo in early October, and the first convoys in nine months, JW54A and B, safely reached the Kola inlet by late November. RA54A also returned without incident.

In December, the next convoy, JW55A, sailed. It arrived safely although it was spotted by German reconnaissance aircraft. Admiral Dönitz finally secured from Hitler the authority to commit his remaining heavy surface units against the Arctic convoys in early 1943. However, given the cessation of the convoys in the summer, there had been little opportunity, and the Kriegsmarine in Norway had been somewhat inactive. Thus the German naval staff issued orders in November stating that: "The functions of the ships remain unaltered... Against this Traffic [the Arctic convoys], both the Northern Task Force [essentially the *Scharnhorst* and the destroyers] and the U-boats are to be employed." Admiral Kummetz, the task force commander, preferred to wait for the completion of the *Tirpitz*'s repairs and restrict himself to forays with the destroyers. However, Dönitz gained Hitler's permission to commit the battle cruiser against the next convoy on December 19, 1943.

He also reinforced the two U-boat flotillas in Norway. With Kummetz on leave, Rear-Admiral Bey, commanding the destroyers, was given the task of attacking the convoy.

On December 20, JW55B sailed from Loch Awe. As well as the normal complement of destroyers, cover was provided by three cruisers under Vice-Admiral Burnett, while distant protection was down to the Commander-in-Chief Home Fleet, Bruce Fraser, aboard the battleship *Duke of York*. The convoy was spotted by a German meteorological flight on December 22. The Luftwaffe rediscovered it on December 25, and soon there was a single U-boat in company, with another seven in the area. Admiral Schniewind, commander of Group North, tried to have the operation postponed in view of inadequate intelligence, but the extreme pressure of the situation on the Eastern Front was pressed upon him, and he ordered that the *Scharnhorst* put to sea on December 25, 1943. British Ultra intelligence revealed the fact to the Royal Navy, and Fraser was informed of the intelligence in the early hours of the following day.

The heavy seas had forced Admiral Bey to detach his destroyer escort. So he was alone when his ship encountered Burnett's cruisers on the morning of December 26. The British sighted the German ship first and opened fire at 9:29 AM, disabling her forward radar. The *Scharnhorst* turned away and used

her superior speed to break contact. Bey made a further attempt to close on the convoy, but was again intercepted by Burnett's ships two hours later. Meanwhile, Fraser on *Duke of York*, in company with the cruiser *Jamaica* and four destroyers, had placed himself between the *Scharnhorst* and her base at Altenfjord. The *Duke of York* picked her up on radar at 4:17 PM, and as the range closed the *Duke of York* and *Jamaica* were able to open fire at 4:50 PM. The *Scharnhorst* was caught unawares and turned north into the path of Burnett. As the *Scharnhorst* tried to open the distance, the battle became a gunfire duel between the two capital ships. Hits from the *Duke of York* slowed the German ship and her firing stopped. The British destroyers then attacked and torpedo hits sealed the *Scharnhorst*'s fate by slowing her further. By 7:30 PM her speed was down to five knots, and Fraser sent in the destroyers and cruisers to finish her off with torpedoes. It is not known when the *Scharnhorst* sank, probably it was about 7:45 PM. Of her crew of 1,903 and 40 cadets, only 36 men were saved.

The sinking of the *Scharnhorst* was an important British victory. The superiority of British radar, their intelligence provided by Ultra, and Fraser and Burnett's handling of their ships had removed the threat of the last enemy capital ship operational in Norway. German mistakes had contributed to the defeat, too. The Luftwaffe had

Below: **The German battleship** Scharnhorst *was sunk in December 1943 by British ships during a foray against an Arctic convoy.*

cooperated poorly with the navy: a seaplane had spotted the British ships, but there had been no swift relay of the information to Bey. Bey himself was inexperienced in capital ship operations. He had said himself when appointed Kummetz's stand-in, "The last time I was aboard a capital ship was as a cadet." The German Navy had been desperate to justify itself, had put to sea in unfavorable conditions, and consequently had been caught by the British. Now with the *Scharnhorst* sunk, the *Tirpitz* immobilized, and the *Lützow* returned to Germany, the most serious menace to the convoys had gone. It was a turning point in the naval war around Norway. From 1941 to the end of 1943, the Royal Navy had been on the defensive, protecting the convoys and ensuring the German surface forces did not break out into the Atlantic Ocean. With the changed situation, the British could go on the offensive, even using the tactically defensive convoys to a strategically aggressive end. Once won, the British never lost the initiative that the Germans had taken from them in April and May 1940. By the end of 1943, therefore, the German Navy in Norway was, to all intents and purposes, beaten.

The removal of the threat of the two German capital ships ended any serious notion of a balanced German fleet. The U-boats remained a potent weapon, but they would never be able to overwhelm and destroy totally an escorted convoy. German air resources in northern Norway were largely limited to reconnaissance aircraft. Yet the *Tirpitz*, sitting in its anchorage at Altenfjord, might still become a threat once more. Repairs were proceeding apace and there was no intention of sending her south. In January, Dönitz even suggested reinforcing her with the *Prinz Eugen*, then in the Baltic. So the Germans might well use her against the convoys, although she was not fully operational. Thus, as her repairs neared completion, the Royal Navy took matters into its own hands, being unable to persuade RAF Bomber Command to attack the German battleship. Gaining complete tactical surprise on the morning of April 3, 1944, Royal Naval carrier-borne Barracudas achieved 14 hits on the *Tirpitz*. Although none of the damage was very serious, the ship was put out of action for a further three months. Dönitz was determined that fresh repairs be made, as he was well aware of the Royal Navy resources she tied down merely as a continued threat.

Below: **Survivors of the** Scharnhorst *on the catapult deck of HMS* Duke of York, *one of the Royal Navy ships that sank the German ship.*

Above: **A victorious homecoming: the battleship** Duke of York *in British home waters after her heroics against the* Scharnhorst.

withdrew, having achieved nothing. The Battle of the Barents Sea was over. There were some losses among the smaller vessels: the Germans lost a destroyer and the British a destroyer and a minesweeper.

The Admiralty was delighted: light forces had driven off a heavy cruiser and a pocket battleship without loss to the convoy. The reaction in Germany was understandably somewhat different. Hitler failed to recognize that it was his own reluctance to risk the heavy ships that had led to the timidity and poor morale of the Kriegsmarine in Norway. Raeder produced a memorandum on the role of the German Navy on January 15, 1943. He pointed out that only a balanced fleet, including capital ships, could tie down the Royal Navy to any degree and prevent it from concentrating its whole strength against the U-boats. Basing the fleet in Norway forced the British to secure the Atlantic convoy route and equip the Home Fleet with the most modern battleships and several

aircraft carriers that could be better used elsewhere.

It was to no avail, however, and Raeder resigned on January 30. Hitler replaced him with Karl Dönitz. Dönitz prepared a scheme to decommission most of the navy's heavy ships. However, he had no intention of following through such a plan and persuaded Hitler to allow him to use the *Scharnhorst* and *Tirpitz* against the convoys without crippling restrictions. As a result, the repaired and reprieved *Scharnhorst* sailed to Norway in March 1943 to join the *Tirpitz* and *Lützow*. They all then sailed to Altenfjord in the extreme north of Norway.

Tirpitz in range

The whole strategic position hung on the *Tirpitz*. There remained no real defense against her if she sortied against an Arctic convoy in earnest. The British had made numerous bombing attempts against the *Tirpitz* in her anchorage in Trondheim, and in October 1942 a joint

Allied merchant ships under attack during the Battle of the Barents Sea. The engagement was a humiliating defeat for the Kriegsmarine.

Special Operations Executive (SOE)/ Royal Navy midget submarine attack had been aborted remarkably close to the target. Since the *Tirpitz*'s move to Altenfjord put it beyond the range of RAF aircraft, the Royal Navy decided to try again, this time using three-man X-Craft submarines. Six of these midget submarines were towed across the North Sea by T and S Class submarines of the Home Flotillas. By September 20, they were in position outside Altenfjord, although only four were able to make the attack, as *X-8* was scuttled and *X-9* was lost with all her crew. The X-Craft reached their objective on September 22. Two of the craft, *X-6*, commanded by Lieutenant Donald Cameron, RNR, and *X-7*, commanded by Lieutenant Godfrey Place, RN, managed to negotiate the *Tirpitz*'s defenses and place their charges beneath her. Cameron and his crew were taken aboard the target and "prior to the explosion it is reported that the crew of *X-6* were seen looking anxiously at their watches." At least two charges went off at 8:30 AM: "The *Tirpitz* was heaved five or six feet [1.5–1.8m] out of the water." The surviving British crews were "well treated and given hot coffee and schnapps." Indeed, the German sailors "expressed great admiration of their bravery." Both Place and Cameron were awarded the Victoria Cross.

The German battleship had been seriously damaged. The 2,000-ton (2,032 metric tonne) "C" turret had been lifted by the explosion and then dropped down and jammed. Dönitz told Hitler of the attack on September 24, and, as he feared for the ship's safety on a journey to Germany, they agreed she should remain in Norway and have repairs made in situ. They hoped to have the major repairs completed by the middle of March 1944. In addition to this, the *Lützow* sailed from Norway for the Baltic on September 26. The Kriegsmarine's strength in Norway was now very much weakened.

With the *Tirpitz* damaged, the Royal Navy became increasing aggressive off the Norwegian coast. As the Arctic

The rail network in Russia was the most reliable form of all-weather transport, particularly in the remote Arctic region. The Soviet officer seated right and his companion are members of a line of communications formation.

convoys had been halted to release shipping for Operation Overlord, the Allied invasion of Normandy, the Royal Navy attempted to harass Norwegian coastal traffic and simulate a threat to Norway as part of the deception plan "Fortitude North."

End game

The British hoped that these operations would encourage the Germans to keep their large U-boat forces in the area rather than use them against the shipping that was supplying Allied forces in Normandy. Once the success of Overlord began to release destroyers for other missions, the British Admiralty considered restarting the Arctic convoys. It was conceivable that a repaired *Tirpitz* might be capable of limited operations against them, however. The main problem was that Fleet Air Arm aircraft could not carry a bomb heavy

enough to seriously damage the ship. So the RAF was the only alternative. Plans were laid, and on September 15, 1944, RAF Lancasters flying out of Yagodnik airfield in Russia carrying 12,000-lb (5,445-kg) Tall Boy bombs attacked the *Tirpitz* at anchor. They achieved a single direct hit, which was enough to blow a hole in her forward deck on the starboard side. The battleship was lucky to still be afloat.

A floating battery

The Red Army launched an offensive in the far north in June 1944, which forced Finland to seek terms. The Finnish–Soviet armistice of September 19 made the German position in northern Norway extremely precarious, as the Soviet advance carried the Red Army into Norwegian Finnmark. At a meeting on September 20, Dönitz and the Naval War Staff concluded that, "it was no longer possible to make the *Tirpitz* ready for sea and action again." Rather than risk towing her back to Germany, they decided to move the ship to Tromso for use as a floating battery against any British landing. The *Tirpitz* moved to her new berth at Tromso on October 15. The Germans rested the only partially seaworthy battleship on a sandbank and surrounded her with anti-aircraft defenses and a double net barrage brought down from Altenfjord. However, the move to Tromso sealed the battleship's fate. Whatever the man-made defenses, there was no protective mountain above the ship as there had been at Trondheim and Altenfjord. More importantly, she was now within range of RAF bombers based in Great

The stability of the Arctic Front made the erection of substantial buildings such as these worthwhile, as well as necessary, given the weather. A plentiful supply of timber for building was readily available. These are Russian lodgings outside Murmansk.

An aerial view of the German battleship Tirpitz in the Narvik-Bogen Fjord, Norway. Tirpitz was based in Norway from early 1942, where it posed a constant threat to Allied convoys.

Britain. She was attacked on October 28 and again on November 12. At 9:40 AM on November 12, the *Tirpitz*'s main armament opened up on the incoming Lancaster bombers. The ship's captain, Robert Weber, frantically requested air cover from Bardufoss airfield, but no aircraft were forthcoming. *Tirpitz* was hit twice and then capsized. About a thousand of her crew were trapped inside; only 85 could be rescued by cutting through the hull.

The *Tirpitz* had been based in Norway for three years, and while she achieved nothing in action, her mere presence had caused the Royal Navy inordinate problems. The possibility of her attacking the Arctic convoys, or breaking into the Atlantic, had had a disproportionate effect on British naval strategy. The Royal Navy had risked and lost valuable cruisers in the Barents Sea, been forced to cancel convoys, and had scattered PQ17 due to the possibility of the battleship attacking.

With the removal of this threat, and the almost total lack of German bomber aircraft in Norway, the Royal Navy was able to dominate the Norwegian coast. The disruption of iron-ore traffic was a useful strategic goal. More important were the Arctic convoys. When the Royal Navy finally gained the upper hand in the Battle of the Atlantic in mid-1943, it shifted to offensive anti-U-boat operations.

With the *Scharnhorst* sunk, the *Tirpitz* crippled, and the Luftwaffe presence in northern Norway much reduced, the U-boats remained the principal threat to the Arctic convoys. Dönitz intended to wait until the introduction of the new Type XXI U-boats before restarting the Atlantic campaign. However, the worsening situation on the Eastern Front and the perceived need to stop the Arctic convoys led the Kriegsmarine

to regard attacks on the convoys as an essentially defensive commitment. Admiral Dönitz therefore increased the number of U-boats in Norway to 33 by moving 20 Atlantic boats there in January 1945, in response to the British restarting the Arctic convoys that month.

> "While the *Tirpitz* achieved nothing in action, her mere presence caused the Royal Navy inordinate problems"

Arctic convoys in retrospect

Historic assessment of the Arctic convoys has usually emphasized their defensive nature. This was certainly true of the period 1941–1943, when the Soviet Union was in serious need of supplies. However, out of the more than 985,000 tons (1,000,000 metric tonnes) of supplies transported to Russia by the convoys in 1944–1945, much remained unused. The convoys were never critical to British survival, and, when more important British interests were at stake, they were suspended. However, the destruction of the German U-boat arm remained a vital strategic goal. Thus the Royal Navy created a battle of attrition in the Arctic that the Germans were forced to fight.

The Arctic was the only area where the U-boats remained in large concentrations. Success in the Atlantic allowed the British to shift experienced anti-submarine warfare forces to the Arctic. The Home Fleet was prepared to commit two or three escort carriers, and the British were reading Enigma easily. The convoys were basically "fought through" to their destination. In the second half of 1944, 159 ships left for Russia, and all arrived safely; 100 set out for home, and only two were lost. The Germans lost nine U-boats. In 1945, the Germans switched tactics, congregating in the Kola inlet rather than forming a patrol line off Bear Island.

THE *TIRPITZ*

The *Tirpitz*—like its sister ship the *Bismarck*—was a leading ship in the Kriegsmarine. It was launched in 1939 and named for Admiral Alfred von Tirpitz, an early commander of the German Navy. The battleship was 830 feet (253 m) long, was powered by 12 boilers and three turbines, and could achieve a speed of over 30 knots. The *Tirpitz*'s armament was formidable, and included eight 15-in main guns, 55 other guns and cannons, and eight torpedo tubes.

For most of the war, the *Tirpitz* was confined to northern harbors because of Hitler's lack of confidence in surface vessels. Its threat to Allied convoys was more imagined than real, but the British pursued it until they destroyed it by air attack on November 12, 1944.

The German battleship Tirpitz *lies capsized in Tromsö Fjord, Norway, in November 1944, following an attack by RAF bombers.*

Royal Navy operations in Norwegian waters had also led to the stationing of increased numbers of Luftwaffe torpedo bombers in the north. Consequently, the convoys during the last six months of the war met with remarkably stiff resistance. Heavy air attacks were launched against JW64 and RA64 and were beaten off with serious Luftwaffe losses. Despite Schnorkel equipped U-boats and a tightening of U-boat signals and the resultant loss of Ultra, U-boat losses were high. Before 1944 the U-boats had sunk one escort, in 1944 they sunk three, and in 1945 a further four. There were also higher mercantile losses, too: no merchantmen were lost in 1943, 11

thereafter. This was judged a reasonable and economic price, though.

The RAF also conducted bombing raids against the U-boat pens at Bergen and Trondheim because the Admiralty was fearful of a new U-boat offensive by superior Type XXI and Type XXIII submarines. It is difficult to judge the effects of these RAF attacks on the U-boat bases in Norway. Had the war continued, and a second U-boat offensive developed using new submarines and technology, the Norwegian bases might have become of crucial importance. However, the Germans never regained the initiative, and with production dislocated by constant RAF and United States Army Air Force (USAAF) bombing, the feared Type XXI did not enter service until April 1945, far too late to affect the outcome of the war.

The last wartime Arctic convoy, JW66, sailed on April 16, 1945, and arrived safely without encountering the enemy. The return convoy, RA66, left Kola on April 29. A preliminary sweep of the inlet accounted for two U-boats, and in the last contact of the war, the frigate HMS *Goodall* was sunk by Lieutenant Westphalen in *U-968*. The Arctic naval war was over.

Norway was of vital importance to Germany in the war at sea. German naval thinking had recognized this since World War I, and *Weserübung* was essentially a Kriegsmarine victory.

Conclusion

Although Norway's strategic importance diminished with the fall of France in 1940, Great Britain's decision to supply the Soviet Union by the Arctic route changed that, as Hitler decided to send his heavy surface units to Norway. German possession of the country gave its forces a whole host of advantages in the convoy battles. Norway sat on the southern flank of a convoy route where the Germans set up a series of excellent sea and air bases, most out of range of or invulnerable to British land-based bombing for the first years of the war.

Once the Germans decided to make a serious effort against the convoys, a pattern became clear. The experience of the early convoys of 1942 showed that the ships could be fought through against the U-boats and German aircraft, albeit often with serious losses, if good convoy discipline was maintained. The *Tirpitz* and other heavy units changed all that. One or more of these ships could overwhelm the destroyer and cruiser escort and thus annihilate the convoy. This was

British Barracudas on their way to attack the Tirpitz *in April 1944. The attack put the battleship out of action for a further three months.*

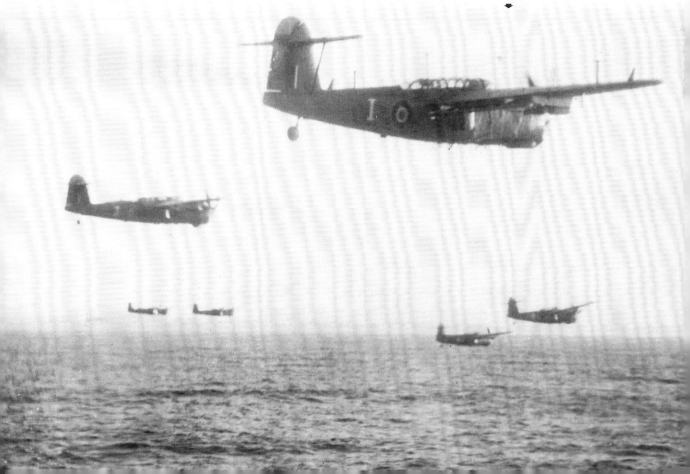

CONVOY PROTECTION

Protecting convoys of merchantmen was crucial for the survival of the United Kingdom during World War II.

The convoy system had been developed during World War I, when German U-boats took a heavy toll on isolated merchantmen. Although a convoy provided a bigger target for U-boats than a single vessel, and their speed was limited to the speed of the slowest ship, the merchantmen could be protected by warships that could counterattack the submarines.

During the Battle of the Atlantic in World War II, there were constant developments in the technology and tactics used to defend convoys. For their part, the Germans also made many changes to their boats and their systems. Convoys usually consisted of between 30 and 70 ships.

The key difference between World War I and World War II was the role of aircraft. On one level this concerned long-range land-based aircraft, but it also involved aircraft being part of the protection system of the convoys themselves. For example, catapult systems for launching fighter aircraft into the air to attack U-boats were placed on some warships and merchant vessels. It was accepted that the aircraft itself would be lost, but it could provide a crucial extra element of cover. Later, small aircraft

carriers were also used to provide very efficient cover.

A whole new class of small warships also came into play to work against U-boats. These were "corvettes"—small craft that carried depth charges and were able to release destroyers for other duties. Corvettes could be produced in large numbers, although they were very uncomfortable for their crews in the Atlantic swell.

Convoys were very vulnerable to German surface raiders (as was shown when the German heavy cruiser *Admiral Scheer* attacked convoy HX-84 in November 1940), but very effective against single U-boats. The Germans had to change their tactics and attack in "Wolf Packs" to seriously threaten well-organized convoys.

The worth of the convoy system was demonstrated clearly in the first six months of 1942. The head of the U.S. Navy, Admiral King, ignored British advice to institute convoys along the U.S. eastern seaboard. The result was what the U-boat crews called a "happy time" until King realized his mistake and brought in convoys.

Above: A convoy escort ship drops depth charges against U-boats. Depth charges were simply drums of explosive dropped into the water, with fuses that set them off at a certain depth. Early depth charges needed to explode within 32 feet (10 m) of a U-boat to destroy it. When the detected a U-boat, escort vessels dropped depth charges patterns, which typically involved 12 depth charges bein used at once. During World War II, 785 German U-boa were sunk by Allied forces.

Above: An Atlantic convoy steams toward Britain. Convoys were restricted in speed. Slow convoys made six knots, while fast convoys made 12 knots. As the war went on, convoys became larger, as large convoys prove easier to defend by concentrating surface warships and aerial protection around big groups of merchantmen. The merchant vessels were usually commanded by a retired admiral from the Royal Navy, while the warship concentrated on fighting the submarine menace.

Below: HMS Audacity was the first aircraft carrier dedicated to convoy protection. She was based on the hull of a captured German merchant vessel, the Hannover. Her aircraft proved very effective, not only against U-boats but also against the Germans' main aerial threat to convoys, the long-range Focke-Wulf Condor bombers. On her final voyage, her aircraft downed four Condors before Audacity herself was torpedoed and sunk in December 1941.

ve: A British Supermarine Seafire, the seaborne
ion of the Spitfire. Important convoys were given escort
iers to help them fight off U-boat attacks.

Right: A U-boat under
attack from the depth
charges and machine
guns of a Short
nderland flying boat.
underlands and other
aircraft were deadly
foes of the German
submarine fleet.

w: HMS Bluebell, a Flower-class corvette.
e 259 Flower-class corvettes were built,
33 were sunk during the war. These
ettes had crews of 85 men and were armed
a single 4-in gun, light-caliber anti-aircraft
pons, and, most importantly, 70 depth
ges for use against submarines.

spectacularly demonstrated by the scattering of PQ17 caused by the mere possibility of the sailing of the *Tirpitz*. The lengths the British went to sink the *Tirpitz* are therefore hardly surprising. Her presence alone forced them to keep battleships and aircraft carriers in the Home Fleet.

A war of attrition

Yet even once their heavy units were sunk or crippled, the Germans still had to attack the convoys. They perceived a direct link between the Allied supplies getting through and the progress of the war on the Eastern Front. Similarly, German naval historians calculate that the 500,000 vehicles that arrived in Murmansk between August 1944 and April 1945 were vital to enabling the Soviets to equip some 60 additional motorized divisions. So, even in 1945, the Germans had to send their limited resources out against the convoys and fight a battle of attrition that was to the Royal Navy's advantage.

The Royal Navy reckoned that, had the positions been reversed, they would have destroyed every Arctic convoy. Indeed, considering the resources available to the Germans in surface craft, submarines, and aircraft, it is almost inexplicable they did not cause the British far worse problems in the Arctic. The indecisive use of the Kriegsmarine was due to poor leadership from Hitler downward. The Führer placed crippling limits on his major surface units and had no sound concept of their use. His hesitancy sapped morale and created a cautious attitude. When the ships were used, their commanders showed considerable timidity, as at the Battle of the Barents Sea, or incompetence, such as when the *Scharnhorst* was sunk.

CHAPTER 3
THE BATTLE OF THE ATLANTIC: 1942–1945

By 1941, the wolf packs of German U-boats in the Atlantic had proved to be one of the greatest threats to the British war effort. In 1942, the United States would also experience the horror of the U-boat war.

Previous pages: A mine scores a direct hit on a U-boat. U-boats traveling on the surface were vulnerable to air attack.

A British ship burns after being hit by a Luftwaffe bomb on the Arctic convoy route. The convoys took supplies from Britain to Soviet Russia's northern ports, principally Murmansk.

In late 1941, the British were beginning to make some headway in countering the U-boat threat. Merchant-shipping losses remained high, with about 400,000 tons (406,500 metric tonnes) sunk during November, but the figure had fallen from a peak of 900,000 tons (914,442 metric tonnes) during the summer.

U-boats, once nearly invulnerable, now faced real danger from rapid British convoy escorts that used barrages of depth charges, or underwater bombs. New sonar technology known as Asdic increased depth-charge accuracy. In addition, better radar introduced in early 1941 enabled an escort to detect a surfaced U-boat up to 1.75 miles (3 km) away.

Progress was also being made in deciphering the German Enigma military codes. As a result, more convoys could avoid wolf packs—groups of U-boats—and their escorts were better prepared. Convoys were also helped by air support from escort aircraft carriers and long-range anti-submarine aircraft. In addition, new convoy shipping provided by the U.S. Lend–Lease policy helped to turn the tables on the U-boats in the Battle of the Atlantic.

Until December 7, 1941, the United States was technically neutral in the war. However, the Japanese attack on Pearl Harbor and Hitler's subsequent declaration of war on the United States changed the Atlantic War entirely.

Operation Drumbeat

The commander of the U-boat fleet, Karl Dönitz, saw new opportunities. He started Operation Drumbeat, diverting much of his force from the central Atlantic to patrol the eastern coast of the United States. The U.S. homeland had so far been untouched by war, and a mixture of complacency and inexperience was to have tragic results. The merchant fleet that sailed along the U.S. coast was almost entirely unprotected.

On January 12, 1942, *U-123*, commanded by Reinhard Hardegan, moved into waters off the northern United States. It sank the merchantman *Cyclops* off Nova Scotia; two nights later the tanker *Norness* was destroyed 60 miles (96 km) off Long Island, New York.

Hardegan then took his craft deeper into New York waters: at one stage he could see the bright lights of New York City. Over subsequent months, U-boat commanders benefited from coastal lights, which had the effect of silhouetting targets clearly. The U.S. authorities initially refused to implement blackouts like those used in Britain. As losses mounted, they applied a "dim-out," in which lights were dimmed rather than turned off. From offshore, however, any onshore illumination made targets stand out prominently enough to help the U-boats.

The return of the "Happy Time"

Spurred by Hardegan's successes (he sank another tanker on January 15), Dönitz deployed more U-boats to similar positions. Before long, 12 U-boats were on patrol along the East Coast at any one time. From January to June, 327 U.S. ships were sunk in U.S. waters between Maine and the Caribbean. Some 1.25 million tons (1.27 million metric tonnes) of ships were lost in the first three months of the year, and a similar total in May and June. More than 2,400 sailors died, and U.S. coastal communities experienced dead bodies washing up on their shores.

Arguing from experience, the British advised the U.S. chief of naval operations, Admiral Ernest J. King, to group ships into convoys protected by heavy escorts. King instead tried measures such as anti-submarine patrols and decoy shipping. The rising losses were a convincing argument, however, and by July 1942, the United States had adopted convoy systems.

Eyewitness Report:

" There is a frightful crack, just as if the boat has been struck by a gigantic hammer. Electric bulbs and glasses fly about, leaving fragments everywhere. The motors have stopped. Reports from all stations show, thank God, that there are no leaks—just the main fuses blown. The damage is made good. We are now using special breathing apparatus to guard against the deadly carbon-monoxide which may be in the boat. The rubber mouthpiece tastes horrible. "

Midshipman Heinz Schaefer, on *U-977*, as it is depth-charged in the mid-Atlantic, 1942

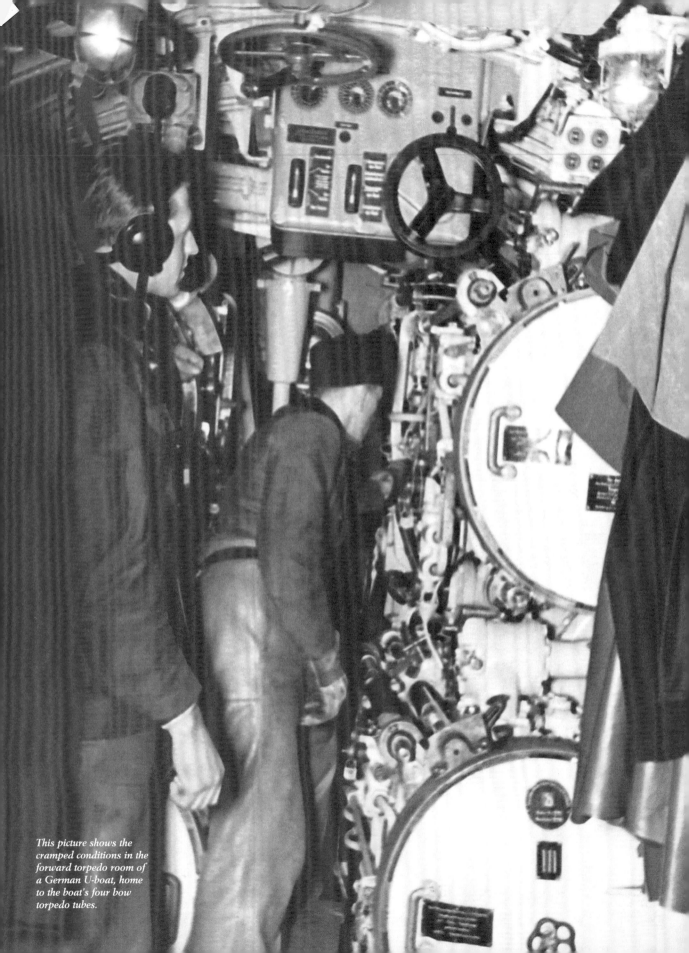

This picture shows the cramped conditions in the forward torpedo room of a German U-boat, home to the boat's four bow torpedo tubes.

THE ST. NAZAIRE RAID

In the spring of 1942, in order to prevent the German battleship *Tirpitz* from operating in the Atlantic, the British planned to destroy the dry dock at St. Nazaire in France on which the battleship would rely. The plan was to ram the dock gate with an old destroyer packed with explosives armed with delayed fuses. Meanwhile, commandos would demolish key shore installations.

On March 26, 1942, HMS *Campbeltown*, packed with explosives, sailed for St. Nazaire with 18 other vessels. At 1:34 AM on March28, under fire from coastal guns, it rammed the dock gates. The commandos destroyed many installations, but the evacuation went wrong. Only 227 of the 611 raiders returned to Britain. At around 11:35 AM, *Campbeltown* exploded with a huge detonation that killed 360 Germans and wrecked the harbor. The dock was unusable for the rest of the war.

Campbeltown *exploded 10 hours after ramming the dock at St. Nazaire.*

However, Operation Drumbeat and further attacks on convoys in the Atlantic resulted in between 6 million and 8 million tons (6.1 million and 8.1 million metric tonnes) of Allied shipping losses in 1942. The U-boat commanders referred to this period of success as their second "Happy Time."

Exploiting the weak spots

The U.S. shipbuilding industry, however, had geared up to produce more ships than the U-boat fleet could sink. A "Liberty" ship—a standard, prefabricated merchant vessel—could be produced in three months or much less. The record was less than five days. By the end of October 1942, three Liberty ships or their tanker equivalent, the T10, were being completed almost every day.

In response to convoy tactics being used along the East Coast, in August 1942 Dönitz switched his focus to the so-called Atlantic air gap, a large stretch of the ocean that lay beyond the range of Allied land-based anti-submarine aircraft. Over subsequent months, too, much Allied escort and merchant shipping was relocated to operations in North Africa, leaving the Atlantic convoys even more vulnerable.

Two huge packs of U-boats now patrolled just within the borders of the air gap, aiming to catch Allied convoys as they entered and exited. By March 1943, a total of 240 U-boats were in the central Atlantic. Their range was increased as specialist refueling submarines were developed. Meanwhile, German naval codes were changing and again defeating the Allied decoding efforts.

The level of merchant sinkings rose again, from 300,000 tons (304,800 metric tonnes) in February to 476,000 tons (484,000 metric tonnes) in March. But the second Happy Time could not last. The U.S. convoy system steadily began to make life harder for the U-boats. About 15 U-boats were being built every month, but a similar number were being sunk.

The British tanker SS Empire Gem, carrying gasoline from the United States to Britain, sinks after being struck by a German torpedo south of Cape Hatteras, North Carolina, in January 1942.

received better weaponry since late 1942. In addition to depth charges, which sank 43 percent of all destroyed U-boats, many escort vessels were also armed with the "hedgehog." This weapon fired 24 small bombs that sank through the water in a circular pattern 130 feet (40 m) in diameter; the bombs exploded on contact with an enemy craft. Later in 1943, the British introduced the "squid," a three-barrelled mortar that fired fast-sinking bombs set to explode at a specific depth in a triangular pattern. The bombs hit a U-boat with shockwaves from every side. Escort destroyers also received improved radar and other submarine-locating systems, including "huff-duff", or High Frequency/ Direction Finding (HF/DF) equipment.

The increased U-boat sinkings were the result of rapid developments in anti-submarine tactics and technology. Convoy escorts had

Crewmen from a German U-boat scan the waters for survivors from an Allied freighter they torpedoed the previous day.

This located submarines by picking up their radio transmissions.

Technological advances

While shipboard weapons improved, so too did airborne anti-submarine tactics and firepower. Allied air power in the Atlantic War consisted mainly of Liberator bombers and Sunderland and Catalina flying boats. Armed with depth charges, machine guns, and cannons, the aircraft took a fearsome toll on U-boats within their range.

Aircraft initially discovered submarines either by visual reconnaissance or by radio information from escort ships. However, new centimetric radar systems were installed on board Liberators from spring 1942. They gave aircrews the ability to precisely locate a submarine on the surface.

In May 1943, Very Long Range (VLR) Liberators were introduced in the Atlantic theater. With a range of over 3,000 miles (4,800 km), they closed the mid-Atlantic air gap. Escort carriers were also available in increased numbers, giving convoys air cover for the entire Atlantic crossing. From May 1943, Allied code-breakers again dominated the German naval codes, revealing the submarines' deployment. Even darkness could not conceal the U-boats: Allied aircraft were equipped with powerful search lights that could illuminate the ocean once a U-boat had been detected by radar.

From April 1943, U.S. aircraft also began dropping the Mark 24 Mine, a revolutionary anti-submarine torpedo. Once dropped into the water, the mine would guide itself to the target by homing in on the submarine's propeller noise. With a range of over 11,800 feet (3,600 m), it was a devastating weapon.

The German reaction

Losses among the U-boats became catastrophic; 47 were sunk in May

A U-boat in heavy seas in the North Atlantic, May 1943. May was a decisive month as the mid-Atlantic air gap was closed by very-long-range Liberator bombers.

Survivors from the U.S. steamer Carlton, *one of the ships in the PQ17 convoy, sunk on July 5, 1942, by* U-88.

1943 alone. With such unsustainable losses, Dönitz pulled his U-boat fleet back to France by the end of the year. After the invasion of France in June 1944, however, the Allies seized many submarine stations along the French

coast, as well as sinking a significant number of U-boats. Allied air forces also struck at the core of the U-boat production and transportation network, preventing new submarines from being built or delivered.

The German pocket battleship Gneisenau *was active against British commerce in the Atlantic. She was decommissioned in July 1942 and her turrets removed for coastal defense.*

A crewman struggles across the deck as his U-boat begins to sink.

In response to their losses, the Germans invested in their own new technology. They introduced the "snorkel" air-breathing system. This sucked in air from the surface down a long tube, allowing a U-boat to remain submerged for longer. They also introduced their own homing torpedoes. In February 1945, a new submarine type, the XXIII, came into service. It had an exceptional underwater performance. However, these measures were too late: in May 1945, the navy surrendered with the rest of the German forces.

The U-boat crews suffered the highest percentage of deaths of any arm of service in the German military. Nearly 26,000 U-boat crewmen died out of a total of 40,900 who served; another 5,000 were taken prisoner.

The Arctic war

From August 1941, the Atlantic War was accompanied by another bitter naval conflict being fought to the north and west. This was the war of the Arctic convoys, which sailed from Britain and Iceland by way of the Barents Sea to supply the Soviet Union. While the Atlantic War was mainly a conflict between German U-boats and Allied surface vessels and aircraft, in the Arctic War the Germans combined aviation, U-boats, and surface vessels.

The Arctic convoys were responsible for delivering vast quantities of U.S. and British goods to the Soviet Union. This had been supported by Britain following the German invasion of Russia in June 1941. Over the course of the war, 4.3 million tons (4.36 million metric tonnes) of jeeps, trucks, aircraft, tanks, weapons, boots, and other materiel reached Soviet forces by convoys that sailed to the ports of Archangel, Murmansk, and Molotovsk. The convoys delivered more than 22 percent of the Lend–Lease supplies sent to the Soviet Union and were vital to the Soviet war effort. The first convoy sailed for Russia on August 21, 1941. Each was given a number and two letters: PQ indicated that the convoy was outbound, while QP designated homeward convoys.

Action in the Arctic theater

The first problem for the convoys was the environment. In the hostile Arctic waters, air temperatures were often below zero, causing the ships to ice up, and huge storms were common, especially in winter.

On the other hand, enemy action remained relatively light until the spring of 1942, when the German land campaign in Russia ground to a halt.

The second problem was the determination of German aircraft, U-boats, and surface vessels, such as the battleship *Tirpitz*, to intercept the convoys. One convoy, PQ-17, was almost totally destroyed by German attack. But as in the main Atlantic struggle, the Allies gradually came out on top, ensuring a flow of equipment to the Soviet Union and grinding down the German forces.

LONG-RANGE AIRCRAFT

Long-range aircraft played a vital role in the war against the U-boats.

The German submarine fleet was most vulnerable when traveling on the surface to get to its positions in the Atlantic. The conquest of France in 1940 gave the U-boats the priceless gift of a much shorter voyage to get to the central Atlantic, while in the Atlantic itself there was also a "gap" early in the war which Allied aircraft could not effectively patrol.

British Coastal Command used various aircraft against the U-boats: early in the war, the Short Sunderland flying boat was an important workhorse. However, the war between U-boats and the Allied aircraft stalking them took a decisive turn in 1941, when it was decided to give Coastal Command some U.S.-built Liberator bombers. These aircraft, designated Very Long Range (VLR), enormously extended the area that could be patrolled. Because of competition for scarce resources from Bomber Command, Coastal Command was allocated just one unit of Liberators—No 120 Squadron—over the next year. Nevertheless, they proved very successful, and many more Liberators were allocated to

Coastal Command in 1943. Liberators sank 72 U-boats during the war.

A second aircraft that was very valuable in this role was the Catalina flying boat. By 1943, U-boats were well armed with anti-aircraft guns, and two Victoria Crosses were won by Catalina pilots pressing home their attacks on U-boats in the face of heavy fire. Catalinas destroyed 40 U-boats in all.

These long-range aircraft sacrificed a certain amount of armament in order to lengthen their flying time, and this meant that U-boat anti-aircraft guns were a real threat. But other developments helped the Allies, such as the introduction in early 1943 of Torpex-filled depth charges that would sink to a set depth and then explode. Ultra-bright searchlights known as "Leigh Lights" were also fitted to aircraft to enable them to attack at night.

The main advantage enjoyed by Allied air units was undoubtedly radar. Try as they might, the Germans were always one step behind in combating radar technology, and this cost the U-boats dearly.

Above: Short Sunderland flying boats of Coastal Command. They carried eight .303-in machine guns, but their main weapon against U-boats was the depth charge. Their range of 2,500 miles (4,000 km) gave them the ability to remain over the Atlantic for long periods.

Right: A Lockheed Ventura, one of the aircraft used by Coastal Command until it could get sufficient numbers of the more effective Sunderland and Liberator. With a range of just 1,625 miles (2,600 km), the Ventura was unable to cover the "Atlantic Gap."

Left: A B-24 Liberator. When it came into service, the Liberator had a range of 2,812 miles (4,500km), longer than any other aircraft. This great range was partly due to the design of the slender wings, placed high on the fuselage. But the Liberator was also difficult for inexperienced pilots to fly.

Below: A Consolidated Catalina. With its astonishing range—3,570 miles (5,715 km)—the Catalina was an invaluable weapon in the maritime armory of the Allies. However, its bomb load was only about half that of the Liberator.

Left above: A Vickers Wellington being "bombed up." Wellingtons had a range of 1,875 miles (3,000 km) and were used in increasing numbers by Coastal Command during the war to attack submarines in areas near Britain, such as the Bay of Biscay. The GR.Mk VIII Wellington entered service in spring 1942 and proved very successful against submarines, especially when fitted with the powerful "Leigh Light" for night attacks.

Left below: A Supermarine Walrus, which was catapulted from naval vessels, and which, because it was a seaplane, could be rescued after a patrol. However, the type was unsuitable for attacking U-boats, and in the end became an air–sea rescue aircraft.

SEPTEMBER 1
POLAND
A German force of 53 divisions, supported by 1,600 aircraft, crosses the German and Slovak borders into Poland in a pincer movement. World War II has begun.

SEPTEMBER 3
BRITAIN AND FRANCE
Britain and France declare war on Nazi Germany after the Nazis ignore their demands to immediately withdraw from Poland.

SEPTEMBER 9
POLAND
A Polish counterattack is launched over the Bzura River against Germany's Eighth Army. It only achieves short-term success. The Polish Army is rapidly falling to pieces under the relentless German attacks.

SEPTEMBER 17–30
POLAND
In accordance with a secret pact with Germany, the Soviet Red Army invades Poland. Little resistance is encountered on Poland's eastern border as the Polish Army is fighting for its life to the west.

SEPTEMBER 18–30
POLAND
Poland is defeated and split into two zones of occupation divided by the Bug River. Germany has lost 10,572 troops, and the Soviet Union has 734 men killed in the campaign. Around 50,000 Poles are killed and 750,000 captured.

SEPTEMBER 29
SOVIET UNION
After occupying Poland, the Soviet Union concentrates on extending its control over the Baltic Sea region. During the next few weeks, it gains bases and signs "mutual assistance" agreements with Lithuania, Latvia, and Estonia. Finland, however, will not agree to the Soviet Union's demands and prepares to fight.

OCTOBER 14
SEA WAR, NORTH SEA
The British battleship *Royal Oak* is sunk, with 786 lives lost, after *U-47* passes through antisubmarine defenses at Scapa Flow in the Orkneys.

NOVEMBER 30
EASTERN FRONT, FINLAND
A Soviet army of over 600,000 men, backed by air and naval power, attacks Finland. Highly-motivated Finnish troops use their familiarity with the terrain and their ability to ski through snow-covered areas to launch hit-and-run raids on Red Army units bogged down in the snow.

DECEMBER 16
FINLAND
The Red Army begins a major new offensive. To compensate for their lack of armor and artillery, the Finns use improvised explosive devices ("Molotov Cocktails," named after the Soviet foreign minister) to destroy enemy tanks.

DECEMBER 13
ATLANTIC OCEAN
British ships fight the German pocket battleship *Graf Spee* at Battle of the River Plate. The *Graf Spee* is scuttled by its crew on the 17th.

1940

MARCH 11
FINLAND
The Treaty of Moscow between Finland and the Soviet Union is agreed, ending the Winter War. Finland retains its independence but has to surrender the Karelian Isthmus and Hangö – 10 percent of its territory. Campaign losses: 200,000 Soviet troops and 25,000 Finns.

APRIL 9
NORWAY/DENMARK
A German invasion force, including surface ships, U-boats, and 1,000 aircraft, attacks Denmark and Norway. Denmark is overrun immediately.

APRIL 14–19
NORWAY
An Allied expeditionary force of over 10,000 British, French, and Polish troops lands in Norway.

MAY 7–10
BRITAIN
Prime Minister Neville Chamberlain is severely criticized over the Norwegian campaign. He resigns and is replaced by Winston Churchill.

MAY 10
THE LOW COUNTRIES
German forces invade the Low Countries. But the main German attack will take place in the south, in the Ardennes region of France.

MAY 12–14
FRANCE
German forces reach the Meuse River and fight their way across at Sedan and Dinant on the 13th. German armor advances westward rapidly, opening a 50-mile (75-km) gap in the Allied line. Allied units retreat to the Channel port of Dunkirk.

MAY 26
FRANCE/BELGIUM
Operation Dynamo, the evacuation of Allied forces from the Dunkirk area, begins using small boats and naval vessels.

MAY 31
UNITED STATES
President Franklin D. Roosevelt launches a "billion-dollar defense program" to bolster the armed forces.

JUNE 1–9
NORWAY
After Britain and France reveal to the Norwegians that they are to begin an evacuation, troops begin to withdraw. King Haakon orders his Norwegians to stop fighting on June 9.

JUNE 3–4
FRANCE
Operation Dynamo ends. The remarkable operation has rescued 338,226 men—two-thirds of them British—from the Dunkirk beaches.

JUNE 16–24
FRANCE
Marshal Henri-Philippe Pétain, the new French president, requests an armistice on the 17th. It is agreed on the 22nd. Germany occupies two-thirds of France, including the Channel and Atlantic coastlines.

JULY 1
ATLANTIC OCEAN
The "Happy Time" begins for U-boat crews as their range is increased now that they have bases in French ports. This lasts until October. U-boat crews inflict serious losses on Allied convoys.

JULY 10
BRITAIN
The Battle of Britain begins. Hermann Göring, the Nazi air force chief, orders attacks on shipping and ports in the English Channel.

JULY 21
SOVIET UNION
The Soviets annex Lithuania, Latvia, and Estonia.

AUGUST 24–25
BRITAIN
The Luftwaffe inflicts serious losses on the Royal Air Force (RAF) during attacks on its main air bases in southeast England, straining the resources of Fighter Command to breaking point in a few days.

AUGUST 26–29
GERMANY
The RAF launches a night raid with 81 aircraft on Berlin following a similar raid on London. Hitler is outraged and vows revenge. German aircraft are redirected to make retaliatory raids on London. This relieves the pressure on Fighter Command's air bases.

SEPTEMBER 7–30
AIR WAR, BRITAIN
Full-scale bombing raids on London—the "Blitz"—begin with 500 bombers and 600 fighters.

OCTOBER 28
GREECE
Italy attacks Greece from Albania. The winter weather limits air support, and thousands die of cold.

NOVEMBER 5
UNITED STATES
President Franklin D. Roosevelt is elected for a third term.

NOVEMBER 11–12
MEDITERRANEAN
At the Battle of Taranto, British torpedo aircraft from the carrier *Illustrious* destroy three Italian battleships and damage two other vessels during the raid on the Italian base.

DECEMBER 9–11
EGYPT
The British launch their first offensive in the Western Desert. The Western Desert Force (31,000) attacks the fortified camps that have been established by the Italians in Egypt. Some 34,000 Italians are taken prisoner as they retreat rapidly from Egypt.

1941

JANUARY 2
POLITICS, UNITED STATES
President Franklin D. Roosevelt announces a program to produce 200 freighters—"Liberty" ships—to support the Allied Atlantic convoys.

FEBRUARY 14
NORTH AFRICA
To aid the faltering Italians, the first units of General Erwin Rommel's Afrika Korps land at Tripoli.

MARCH 11
UNITED STATES
President Franklin D. Roosevelt signs the Lend-Lease Act that allows Britain to obtain supplies without having to immediately pay for them in cash.

APRIL 6–15
YUGOSLAVIA/GREECE
Thirty-three German divisions, with Italian and Hungarian support, invade Yugoslavia from the north, east, and southeast. German forces also attack Greece from the north.

APRIL 17
YUGOSLAVIA
Yugoslavia surrenders to Germany. Immediately, guerrilla forces emerge to resist the Nazi occupation.

APRIL 27
GREECE
German forces occupy Athens. Campaign dead: Greek 15,700; Italian 13,755; German 1,518; and British 900.

MAY 20–22
CRETE
A German force of 23,000 men, supported by 600 aircraft, attacks Crete. The Germans launch the first major airborne operation in history.

MAY 23–27
ATLANTIC OCEAN
British ships find the German battleship *Bismarck* and cruiser *Prinz Eugen* in the Denmark Straits between Iceland and Greenland. The *Bismarck* sinks the cruiser *Hood* and damages the battleship *Prince of Wales*, but is then sunk.

MAY 28–31
CRETE
Crete falls to the Germans. British losses are 1,742 men, plus 2,011 dead and wounded at sea, while Germany has 3,985 men killed.

JUNE 22
SOVIET UNION
Germany launches Operation Barbarossa, the invasion of the Soviet Union, with three million men divided into three army groups along a 2000-mile (3200-km) front. Army Group North strikes toward the Baltic and Leningrad. Army Group Center aims to take Smolensk and then Moscow. Army Group South advances toward the Ukraine and the Caucasus.

JULY 31
GERMANY
Reinhard Heydrich, Germany's security chief and head of the SS secret police, receives orders to begin creating a draft plan for the murder of the Jews, which becomes known as the "Final Solution."

SEPTEMBER 30
SOVIET UNION
Operation Typhoon, the German attack on Moscow, officially begins.

NOVEMBER 26
PACIFIC OCEAN
The Japanese First Air Fleet leaves the Kurile Islands on a mission to destroy the U.S. Pacific Fleet at Pearl Harbor, Hawaii.

DECEMBER 7
HAWAII
The Japanese attack Pearl Harbor. Over 183 Japanese aircraft destroy six battleships and 188 aircraft, damage or sink 10 other vessels, and kill 2,000 servicemen. The Japanese lose 29 aircraft.

DECEMBER 8
UNITED STATES
The United States declares war on Japan in retaliation for the attack on Pearl Harbor.

DECEMBER 11
AXIS
Germany and Italy declare war on the United States.

1942

JANUARY 10–11
DUTCH EAST INDIES
A Japanese force begins attacking the Dutch East Indies to secure the oil assets of this island-chain.

JANUARY 20
GERMANY
At the Wannsee Conference, Berlin, deputy head of the SS Reinhard Heydrich reveals his plans for the "Final Solution" to the so-called "Jewish problem." Heydrich receives permission to begin deporting all Jews in German-controlled areas to Eastern Europe to face either forced labor or extermination.

FEBRUARY 8–14
SINGAPORE
Japanese troops capture Singapore. Japan has fewer than 10,000 casualties in Malaya. British forces have lost 138,000 men.

APRIL 9
PHILIPPINES
Major General Jonathan Wainright, commanding the U.S. and Filipino forces, surrenders to the Japanese.

APRIL 18
JAPAN
Lieutenant Colonel James Doolittle leads 16 B-25 bombers, launched from the carrier *Hornet*, against targets in Japan, including Tokyo.

JUNE 4
PACIFIC OCEAN
The Battle of Midway begins. Japan's Admiral Chuichi Nagumo aims to seize the U.S. base at Midway and then destroy the U.S. Pacific Fleet. Japan deploys 165 vessels, including eight carriers. The U.S. Navy has a smaller force but has three carriers. The loss of half of its carrier strength in the battle, plus 275 aircraft, puts Japan on the defensive in the Pacific.

JUNE 21
LIBYA
After the Allied withdrawal into Egypt, the Tobruk garrison falls following German land and air attacks.

JUNE 28
SOVIET UNION
Germany launches its summer offensive, Operation Blue, with its Army Group South attacking east from Kursk toward Voronezh.

JULY 4–10
SOVIET UNION
The siege of Sevastopol ends with the Germans capturing 90,000 men.

AUGUST 7–21
GUADALCANAL
The U.S. 1st Marine Division lands on Guadalcanal Island to overwhelm the Japanese garrison.

SEPTEMBER 2
POLAND
The Nazis are "clearing" the Jewish Warsaw Ghetto. Over 50,000 Jews have been killed by poison gas or sent to concentration camps.

OCTOBER 23
EGYPT
The Battle of El Alamein begins. An attack by 195,000 Allied troops against 104,000 Axis men begins.

NOVEMBER 2–24
EGYPT / LIBYA
Rommel, severely lacking supplies, decides to withdraw from El Alamein.

Germany and Italy have lost 59,000 men killed, wounded, or captured. The Allies have suffered 13,000 killed, wounded, or missing.

NOVEMBER 19
SOVIET UNION
General Zhukov launches a Soviet counteroffensive at Stalingrad to trap the Germans in a massive pincer movement.

1943

FEBRUARY 2
SOVIET UNION
The siege of Stalingrad ends. Field Marshal Friedrich Paulus and 93,000 German troops surrender.

FEBRUARY 14–22
TUNISIA
In the Battle of Kasserine Pass, Rommel's forces cause panic among U.S. troops. He loses 2,000 men; the Americans 10,000.

APRIL 17
GERMANY
The U.S. Eighth Army Air Force attacks Bremen's aircraft factories from its bases in eastern England. Sixteen of the 115 B-17 Flying Fortress bombers from the raid are lost.

MAY 13
TUNISIA
Axis forces surrender. Some 620,000 casualties and prisoners have been sustained by Germany and Italy. Allied campaign losses: French 20,000; British 19,000; and U.S. 18,500.

JULY 5
SOVIET UNION
Over 6,000 German and Soviet tanks and assault guns take part in the Battle of Kursk.

JULY 9
SICILY
U.S. and British troops begin the attack on Sicily.

JULY 12–13
SOVIET UNION
At Kursk, the Soviets launch a counter-offensive around Prokhorovka, and an enormous tank battle develops. The German offensive is defeated.

AUGUST 11–17

SICILY

The Germans finally start withdrawing before U.S. forces enter Messina on the 17th.

SEPTEMBER 9

ITALY

Lieutenant General Mark Clark's U.S. Fifth Army, plus the British X Corps, lands in the Gulf of Salerno.

SEPTEMBER 25

SOVIET UNION

The Soviets recapture Smolensk in their continuing offensive. Germany's Army Group Center is now falling back in some disarray.

NOVEMBER 6

SOVIET UNION

The Soviets recapture Kiev.

DECEMBER 26

ARCTIC OCEAN

At the Battle of the North Cape, the German battleship *Scharnhorst* is sunk.

1944

JANUARY 14–27

SOVIET UNION

The Red Army ends the German blockade of Leningrad. Some 830,000 civilians have died during the siege.

JANUARY 22

ITALY

Troops of the Allied VI Corps make an amphibious landing at Anzio, behind the German lines.

MARCH 7–8

BURMA / INDIA

Operation U-Go, the Japanese offensive to drive the Allies back into India by destroying their bases at Imphal and Kohima, begins.

MARCH 20–22

ITALY

Despite further frontal attacks by New Zealand troops, the German defenders repulse all efforts to dislodge them from Monte Cassino.

MAY 18

ITALY

The Allies capture the monastery of Monte Cassino.

JUNE 6

FRANCE

The Allies launch the greatest amphibious operation in military history—D-Day. Some 50,000 men land on five invasion beaches to establish a toehold in Normandy. Allied casualties are 2,500 dead.

JUNE 19–21

PHILIPPINE SEA

Battle of the Philippine Sea. Japan's Combined Fleet is defeated by the U.S. Fifth Fleet. The Japanese lose 346 aircraft and two carriers. U.S. losses are 30 aircraft and slight damage to a battleship.

JUNE 22

SOVIET UNION

The Red Army launches Operation Bagration against Germany's Army Group Center.

JULY 20

GERMANY

An attempt is made by German officers to assassinate Adolf Hitler. It fails to kill the Führer.

AUGUST 1

POLAND

The Warsaw uprising begins. Some 38,000 soldiers of the Polish Home Army battle with about the same number of German troops.

AUGUST 25

FRANCE

The commander of the German garrison of Paris, General Dietrich von Choltitz, surrenders to the Allies.

SEPTEMBER 17

HOLLAND

Operation Market Garden, an Allied armored and airborne thrust across Holland to outflank the German defenses, begins. Paratroopers land at Arnhem, Eindhoven, and Nijmegen to capture vital bridges.

SEPTEMBER 22–25

HOLLAND

The paratroopers fall back from Arnhem, leaving 2,500 dead behind.

OCTOBER 2

POLAND

The last Poles in Warsaw surrender as the Germans crush the uprising. Polish

deaths number 150,000. The Germans have lost 26,000 men.

OCTOBER 20

PHILIPPINES

As the U.S. Sixth Army lands on Leyte Island, General Douglas MacArthur wades ashore and keeps a promise he made two years earlier: "I shall return."

OCTOBER 23–26

PHILIPPINES

Following the U.S. landings on Leyte, the Japanese Combined Fleet is defeated at the Battle of Leyte Gulf.

DECEMBER 16–22

BELGIUM

Hitler launches Operation Watch on the Rhine, his attempt to capture Antwerp. The thick fog means the Germans achieve complete surprise. But they fail to capture Bastogne.

1945

JANUARY 9

PHILIPPINES

The U.S. Sixth Army makes unopposed amphibious landings on Luzon.

JANUARY 27

POLAND

The Red Army liberates the Nazi death camp at Auschwitz.

JANUARY 28

BELGIUM

The last bits of the German "bulge" in the Ardennes are wiped out. The Germans have lost 100,000 killed, wounded, and captured in their defeat. The Americans have lost 81,000 killed, wounded, or captured, and the British 1,400 killed.

JANUARY 30

GERMANY

The Red Army is only 100 miles (160 km) from Berlin.

FEBRUARY 4–11

SOVIET UNION

Marshal Joseph Stalin, President Franklin D. Roosevelt, and Prime Minister Winston Churchill meet at the Yalta Conference in the Crimea to discuss postwar Europe. The "Big Three" decide that Germany will be divided into four zones, administered by Britain, France, the United States, and the Soviet Union.

FEBRUARY 13–14
GERMANY
The RAF mounts a night raid on Dresden. The 805 bombers inflict massive damage on the city, killing 50,000 people.

FEBRUARY 17
IWO JIMA
Under the command of Lieutenant General Holland M. Smith, the U.S. Marines land on the island of Iwo Jima. The attackers are hit by intense artillery and small-arms fire from the 21,000-man Japanese garrison.

MARCH 16
IWO JIMA
The island of Iwo Jima is declared secure by the Americanst. They have lost 6,821 soldiers and sailors dead, while of the 21,000 Japanese garrison, only 1,083 are taken prisoner.

MARCH 22–31
GERMANY
The Allied crossings of the Rhine River begin. German resistance is negligible.

APRIL 1
OKINAWA
Operation Iceberg, the U.S. invasion of the island, commences. The island, only 325 miles (520 km) from Japan, has two airfields on the western side and two partially-protected bays on the east coast—an excellent springboard for the proposed invasion of the Japanese mainland.

APRIL 7
PACIFIC OCEAN
The Japanese *Yamato*, the world's largest battleship, is sunk at sea during an attack by U.S. warplanes.

APRIL 9
ITALY
The final campaign in Italy begins as the U.S. Fifth and British Eighth Armies attack the Germans.

APRIL 12
UNITED STATES
President Franklin D. Roosevelt dies of a cerebral hemorrhage. Vice President Harry S. Truman takes over the position of president.

APRIL 16
GERMANY
The Soviet offensive to capture Berlin commences with a total of 2.5 million men, 41,600 guns and mortars, 6,250 tanks and self-propelled guns, and 7,500 combat aircraft. The Germans have one million men, 10,400 guns and mortars, 1,500 tanks or assault guns, and 3,300 combat aircraft.

APRIL 27
GERMANY
"Fortress Berlin" has been reduced to an east-to-west belt 10 miles (16 km) long by three miles (5 km) wide. German forces within the city are affected by widespread desertions and suicides.

APRIL 28
ITALY
Former Italian dictator Benitto Mussolini and his mistress Claretta Petacci are captured by partisans. They are both shot.

APRIL 30
GERMANY
Adolf Hitler and Eva Braun commit suicide in the Führerbunker in Berlin.

MAY 2
GERMANY
Following a savage three-day battle, in which half the garrison has been killed, Berlin, the capital of Nazi Germany, falls to the Red Army.

MAY 3
BURMA
Following 38 months of Japanese occupation, Rangoon falls to the Allies without a fight.

JUNE 22
OKINAWA
All Japanese resistance on the island ends. The Japanese have lost 110,00 killed during the fighting. The U.S. Tenth Army has suffered 7,613 men killed or missing, and 31,807 wounded.

JULY 17–AUGUST 2
GERMANY
The Potsdam Conference takes place in Berlin. The "Big Three"—U.S. President Harry Truman, Soviet leader Marshal Joseph Stalin, and British Prime Minister Clement Attlee (who had defeated Churchill in a general election on July 5)—meet to discuss postwar

policy. Japan is informed that an immediate surrender would result in the continued existence of its nation, but further resistance will lead to the "utter devastation of the Japanese homeland." This is a veiled reference to the use of atomic weapons against Japan itself.

AUGUST 6
JAPAN
The B-29 Superfortress *Enola Gay* drops an atomic bomb on the Japanese city of Hiroshima, killing 70,000 people and wounding 100,000.

AUGUST 9
MANCHURIA
A massive Soviet offensive by 1.5 million men begins against the Japanese Kwantung Army.

AUGUST 9
JAPAN
A second U.S. atomic bomb is dropped on Nagasaki. It kills 35,000 people and injures a further 60,000.

AUGUST 10
JAPAN
Following a conference, during which the emperor voices his support for an immediate acceptance of the Potsdam Proclamation, Japan announces its willingness to surrender unconditionally.

AUGUST 23
MANCHURIA
The campaign in Manchuria ends in total Soviet victory. The Japanese have lost over 80,000 dead and 594,000 taken prisoner. Soviet losses are 8,000 men killed and 22,000 wounded. The Kwantung Army has been destroyed.

SEPTEMBER 2
ALLIES
Aboard the battleship *Missouri* in Tokyo Bay, Japanese officials sign the Instrument of Surrender, bringing World War II to a close.

GLOSSARY

Allies One of the two groups of combatants in the war. The main Allies were Britain, the Soviet Union, the United States, British Empire troops, and free forces from occupied nations.

armistice An arranged halt in the fighting, usually in preparation for a peace agreement.

attrition A policy of wearing down the enemy by attacking its equipment and personnel.

barrage The coordinated firing of a number of big guns over a period of time.

berth A place at which a ship is anchored.

blockade A barrier set up with ships, mines, or other defenses to prevent ships entering or leaving ports.

capital ship The most powerful type of warship, usually a battleship.

capsize For a vessel to overturn.

commando A soldier trained specifically for raids into enemy-held territory.

convoy A group of ships or vehicles traveling together for protection.

cruiser A medium-sized, well-armed warship.

depth charge An underwater bomb designed to explode when it sinks to a certain depth.

destroyer The smallest and fastest type of warship.

freighter A vessel used to carry cargo.

Lend–Lease A U.S. program that allowed the Allies to buy U.S. military equipment without paying for it until after the war.

maritime Something that is related to the sea.

materiel Any equipment that is used in a military campaign, such as weapons, fuel, or uniforms.

merchantman An unarmed cargo vessel used for trade.

neutral A country that does not take any side in a war.

periscope A long tube with mirrors that allows someone in a submarine to see the surface of the ocean.

radar Equipment that locates objects by bouncing radio waves off them.

reconnaissance Gathering information about the enemy.

scuttle To deliberately sink a ship to prevent it from falling into the hands of the enemy.

snorkel (German: *Schnorkel*) A breathing tube that carries air to a submarine, allowing it to stay submerged for longer.

sonar Equipment that locates underwater objects by sending out sound waves that bounce off them.

sortie A single mission against the enemy.

strategic Something that relates to an overall plan for victory rather than to immediate needs.

task force A group of ships and troops that is put together for a specific purpose.

torpedo A missile that has its own motor.

U-boat Short for *Unterseeboot*, the German name for a submarine.

Ultra The name given to information the Allies learned by breaking German military codes.

FURTHER READING

»»»» BOOKS

Adams, Simon. *World War II* (DK Eyewitness Books). New York, NY: Dorling Kindersley,2007.

De Quesada, Alejandro. *U.S. Coast Guard in World War II*. Oxford, England: Osprey Publishing, 2010.

Gannon, Michael. *Operation Drumbeat: The Dramatic True Story of Germany's First U-boat Attacks Along the American Coast in World War II*. Bethesda, MD: United States Naval Institute, 2009.

Grove, Philip D., Mark J. Grove, and Alastair Finlan. *World War II: The War at Sea* (World War II: Essential Histories). New York, NY: Rosen Publishing Group, 2010.

Jeffrey, Gary. *Battle for the Atlantic* (Graphic Modern History: World War II). New York, NY: Crabtree Publishing Co, 2012.

Morison,Samuel Eliot. *Battle of the Atlantic, September 1939–May 1943* (History of the United States Naval Operations in World War II, vol. 1). Bethesda, MD: Naval Institute Press, 2010.

Shirer, William L. *The Sinking of the Bismarck: The Deadly Hunt*. Boston, MA: Sterling Point Books, 2006.

Taylor, Theodore. *Battle in the Arctic Seas*. Sterling Point Books, 2007.

Tucker, Spencer C. (ed.). *World War II at Sea: An Encyclopedia* (2 vols.). Santa Barbara,CA: ABC-CLIO, 2011.

Wiggins, Melanie. *U-boat Adventures: Firsthand Accounts from World War II*. Bethesda, MD: Naval Institute Press, 2010.

Williamson, Gordon. *Wolf Pack: The Story of the U-boat in World War II*. Oxford, England: Osprey Publishing, 2006.

»»»» WEB SITES

Due to the changing nature of Internet links, Rosen Publishing had developed an online list of websites related to this subject. This site is updated regularly. Please use this link to access the list:

http://www.rosenlinks.com/WW2/Atlan

INDEX